THE COMPLETE
ELECTRIC SMOKER
COOKBOOK

THE COMPLETE
ELECTRIC SMOKER
COOKBOOK

100+ RECIPES AND ESSENTIAL
TECHNIQUES FOR SMOKIN' FAVORITES

BILL WEST

ROCKRIDGE
PRESS

For general information on our other products and services or to obtain technical support, please contact our Customer Care Department within the United States at (866) 744-2665, or outside the United States at (510) 253-0500.

Rockridge Press publishes its books in a variety of electronic and print formats. Some content that appears in print may not be available in electronic books, and vice versa.

Photography © 2021 Iain Bagwell, cover; Hélène Dujardin, pp. ii; Jeff Wasserman/Stocksy, p. vi; The Picture Pantry/Stockfood, pp. ix & 52, back cover; Darren Muir/Stocksy, pp. ix & 174; Bernhard Winkelmann/Stockfood, pp. ix & 92; Borislav Zhuykov/Stocksy, p. 12; Trent Lanz/Stocksy, p. 32; Keller & Keller Photography/Stockfood, p. 72; Dobranska Renata/Stocksy, p. 110; Sabine Steffens/Stockfood, p. 128; Victoria Harley/Stockfood, p. 146; Michael Wissing/Stockfood, p. 160.

Illustration © Tom Bingham, pp. 9 & 20; Monkographic/Shutterstock.com, p. 15.

Hardcover ISBN: 9781638788034 | Paperback ISBN: 978-1-62315-877-4
eBook ISBN: 978-1-939754-76-9

R3

DEDICATED TO MJ WITH ALL MY HEART.

HAPPY WIFE, HAPPY LIFE!

Smoked Corn on the Cob, page 142

CONTENTS

Introduction viii

PART ONE

THE FUNDAMENTALS OF ELECTRIC SMOKING

ONE Going Electric 3

TWO What to Feed Your Smoke 13

PART TWO

LET'S SMOKE SOME MEAT

THREE Poultry 33

FOUR Pork 53

FIVE Beef 73

SIX Fish & Seafood 93

SEVEN Not Your Everyday Barbecue 111

EIGHT Vegetables & Sides 129

NINE Cheese & Nuts 147

TEN Sauces, Rubs & More 161

Measurement Conversions 175

Resources 176

Recipe Index 178

Index 180

INTRODUCTION

ONE HUNDRED AND TEN BUCKS.

Once upon a time, I snatched up a deal on two completely different smokers. I thought the big steal was the mammoth barrel trailer-mounted charcoal grill I was able to claim for just $100. I found it at a church auction where I also picked up a small red electric smoker for just $10. I was totally enamored of the giant hog cooker, as it got me into the game of competition barbecue—and my friends and neighbors were envious. Many hours of repair and a little cash got the beast up to snuff. However, it was the $10 electric smoker that turned out to be the "little engine that could."

The trailer cooker equaled hard work; the Brinkmann electric smoker turned out to be an easy gateway into the world of true smoking. The joy was in the simplicity. No adjustments needed. The single gauge showed warm . . . ideal . . . and hot. No dials or hinges. No switches or buttons. Just a power plug! At first, I actually wondered if the bullet-shaped smoker was even working. It seemed to be heating up, but my caveman brain wanted to see some form of fire! I soon learned the ins and outs of smoking versus grilling. And even with this simple setup, I was able to turn out the best baby backs and pulled pork my family had ever tasted. Experimenting with wood combinations provided that primitive charge I needed through the sight and aroma of roasting pork and wood smoke.

At the same time, I jumped headfirst into barbecue competitions. Electric smokers are not typically allowed and the stakes are high.

You're in a time crunch. Schedules rule the weekend. It's competitive, time-consuming, and expensive. I quickly learned the competition world—live fire, camping out, and countdown clocks—wasn't a hobby I was hungry for (but judging the competition was another story).

My revelation was that I really preferred the simple lifestyle. An electric smoker allowed me to take my eye off the ball (or Boston butt) long enough to do some yard work or honey-dos while simultaneously creating the smoky signal of a great feast to come. Sure, it's a multitasking enabler, but it allows for a stress-free cook. The simplicity of the electric smoker lets you focus on the flavors you're developing and the artistry of that magic combination of time, smoke, and meat.

There's an old saying, "Everyone needs more time, love, and money." Quality barbecue is the same. You need time for low-and-slow cooking. A little love in the prep yields something really special for your guests, and, of course, more money can help you afford quality meat. You don't need your own custom-built smokehouse to turn out the world's best barbecue—just a little time to kill, love for the process, and enough money to buy your main ingredient.

Smoking is best kept simple, so the recipes here use basic ingredients and walk you through the process step by step. (After all, I am a country-radio DJ—I try to keep the words short and few!)

I started with a Brinkmann Gourmet, but whether your electric smoker is made by Masterbuilt, Char-Broil, or Bradley, this complete guide shows you how to smoke your favorite feast authentically, traditionally, and deliciously.

There's plenty of room to geek out, too. Some techniques I provide later in the book have a lot of moving parts. You'll see the special technology behind these machines. Secret ingredients are more fun to share than keep secret for long, so keep reading and you'll discover a few of my favorites in Your Smoking Pantry (page 23).

I hope you're feeling adventurous because in chapter 7 (page 111) we use the humble electric smoker to drop your jaw with a few wonders you may not have expected to smoke. It's anything but boring.

Years after that $10 bullet smoker, I'm sharing food hacks on my food blog BarbecueTricks. On the blog I give tips and tricks to make backyard cooking easier and more delicious. Sometimes the tricks are very complex with multiple steps, but often they're quite simple. And one of the biggest barbecue hacks is to plug in and go electric. Harness the simplicity of low and slow and enhance the flavor by cooking with real wood.

Let's get smokin'.

1

THE FUNDAMENTALS OF ELECTRIC SMOKING

ONE

GOING ELECTRIC

Depending on where you're from, some of your older family members may have practiced the art of smoking in their youth. My mother-in-law remembers the smokehouse at her rural North Carolina home. Curing can be traced back to antiquity, and until the late nineteenth century was the primary way of preserving meat and fish. Curing food by smoking, brining, or salting increases the solute concentration in the food and decreases its water potential. As a result, the food becomes inhospitable to the microbe growth that causes food spoilage.

WHY WE PLUG IN

While meat-preservation processes such as curing were primarily developed to prevent disease and increase food security, the advent of modern preservation methods means that in most developed countries today, curing is mainly practiced for its cultural value and desirable impact on the texture and taste of food. For less-developed countries, curing remains a key process in ensuring the viability of meat production, transport, and access to food.

After curing, some meats are smoked. Smoking is a process that historically involved hanging meats in a smokehouse and letting them absorb the smoke from smoldering fires. This adds flavor and color to meat and slows the development of rancidity. These days it's more about taste and texture than preservation. Still, you need to be mindful of food-safety practices.

Electric smokers, the most recent development in this ancient process, are great choices when it comes to food safety because of their simplicity. That's why I originally fell in love with my first simple Brinkmann Gourmet electric smoker.

Here are the top benefits of electric smokers when it comes to preparing foods safely and reliably.

- The temperature is easily controlled and dependable. Like your home oven, your smoker's electric heating element is built to hold a solid steady temperature.

- The heat is reliable. It won't "go out" accidentally.

- It has a cleaner operation with no need to exchange a lot of charcoal or fuel.

- The stainless steel interior allows for a more sterile environment.

- The sealed cook chambers and modern construction do a better job of keeping out the elements than standard smokers.

THE THREE MUSKETEERS OF ELECTRIC SMOKING

Bradley, Char-Broil, and Masterbuilt are the "Three Musketeers" of electric smoking. All electric smoker models have very similar, and in some cases almost identical, features. Some may have a few important and potentially limiting specialty features (such as for cold-smoking or high-temperature), but there are a few hallmarks of each brand.

Bradley

The Bradley smoker can be spotted a mile away due to its Bradley Bisquette feeding system. These flavor Bisquettes are proprietary to Bradley and do keep you locked into the Bradley brand. The mechanical Bisquette feeder is great for cooks who want quantifiable control of wood and smoke flavor. The Bisquettes are available in 14 "flavors," including the most common smoking woods and some more exotic woods.

The Bradley family of smokers comes in original, digital, and smart versions. Digital versions allow you to dial in an exact temperature while smart smokers allow for remote control from your smartphone.

Char-Broil

Char-Broil, around since 1948, is known for the affordability, solid value, quality, and great design of their smokers. The newer deluxe models include some hi-tech extras such as wireless control and internal thermometers. There is also a tight latch to clasp the door securely. There's something about a chunky latch that makes my inner caveman happy.

Char-Broil also offers variants such as the Simple Smoker. It's the perfect size for smoking that once-a-year Thanksgiving turkey. Additionally, if you're looking to get into the world of wireless control and Bluetooth connectivity with your smartphone, Char-Broil has great options in its digital line. The company has recently stepped up the technology across all their cookers with the SmartChef series—great for the gadget gurus.

Masterbuilt

Masterbuilt boasts a mini-fridge design with a desirable woodchip-loading feature, letting you restock the woodchips without opening the chamber doors, thus not losing any heat. It's a killer feature. Plus, Masterbuilt has a tradition of catering to hunters with the electric (and nonelectric) Sportsman line of smokers.

Other Brands

Other available brands include the primitive bullet electric smoker similar to the one I started with from Brinkmann, plus smokers from Smoke Hollow, Cookshack, and many more that will work with the information and recipes in this book.

A Special Note

You may note that I haven't mentioned REC TEC and Traeger, both of which are pellet cookers. The recipes and smoking information in this book can all work with pellet cookers but haven't been highlighted here for the sole reason that pellet cookers generally cook with heat generated from burning wood pellets and not an electric heating element. I am a big fan of pellet power and write about them a lot on my blog *BarbecueTricks*. They are not officially "electric smokers," but they do use electricity to ignite the pellets, and to power an auger and fan that stokes the intensity of the burning pellets in a small fire pot.

	Bradley Original Smoker	Bradley Smart Smoker with iSmoke Bluetooth	Char-Broil Vertical Electric Smoker	Char-Broil Digital Smoker with SmartChef Wi-Fi	Masterbuilt Digital Electric Smoker 30 Inch	Masterbuilt Bluetooth Smart Digital Smoker 40 Inch
WHEELS	No	2 optional	No	Yes	Optional	Yes
WINDOW	No	No	No	Yes	No	Yes
WATTS	500	500	1,500	750	800	800
PROBE	No	2	No	1	No	Yes
COLOR	Black	Stainless	Black	Stainless	Black	Stainless
NUMBER OF RACKS	4	6, plus optional 4 additional	3	4	4	4
COOK SPACE	520 sq. in.	780 sq. in. (910 sq. in. with the 4 optional racks)	504 sq. in.	721 sq. in.	721 sq. in.	925 sq. in.
PRICE	$269.99	$595	$109	$369	$188	$365
MAX TEMP	280°F	280°F	400°F	275°F	275°F	275°F
WOOD FEEDER	Proprietary Bisquettes	Proprietary Bisquettes	Internal woodchip box	Internal woodchip box	External patented side-loading	External patented side-loading
REMOTE	No	Smartphone app	No	Smartphone app	No	Smartphone app

KNOW YOUR CONTROLS

Each model has different controls. Temperature dials and digital readouts can control the temperature for ideal smoking, but other things also come into play to create that perfect smoked food. As the pit master, your decisions are simple, yet important.

- Choose your preferred recipe and seasoning.

- Preheat the smoker and load your wood of choice for smoke. Note that soaking woodchips in water to prolong smoke and smolder is a debated tactic. In most of the smokers discussed here, soaking the chips is optional or not recommended. For example, soaked or damp Bisquettes in Bradley proprietary units would never work.

- As needed, adjust the target temperature setting to account for external temperature (weather) and wind. Cold weather and driving wind can sometimes prohibit your smoker from holding a steady temperature, even an electric smoker's. Raise the temperature settings a few degrees to compensate. Most of the smokers covered in this book are well insulated and may simply need a bit more time to reach the target temperature when it's cold out.

- Position the food in the smoke chamber for the best heat circulation. Your electric smoker is engineered for even smoke flow, so simply place the food evenly spaced across each rack to avoid blocking the flow. Allow 1 to 2 inches of space around each piece being smoked. Cook temperatures will be a bit hotter closer to the bottom heating element. When cooking entire meals, place larger cuts closer to the heat source and more delicate pieces farther away, for example on the top rack, to ensure more-even cooking.

- Add water to the water pan if desired. While not necessary, water helps create a moist environment, which can be especially useful for preventing large cuts of meat from getting too dry. Bradley smokers do require filling the water pan to extinguish spent Bisquettes. In many smokers, the water pan also helps collect any drippings.

- Let it smoke low and slow and load more wood (for flavor).

- Watch (or check) for your target internal temperature.

Depending on the food you smoke, the ideal smoke or "oven" temperature varies. For example:

- **Cold-smoking foods**, such as cheeses, certain types of fish, nuts, hardboiled eggs, spices, tofu, and even butter, can be done at temperatures below 100°F. By using temperatures this low (or lower), you can infuse delicate foods with distinct wood-smoke flavors without melting or further cooking the food. The smoke can have a curing effect on some proteins, such as salmon, but most of the time cold-smoking is used to add flavor without additional cooking that would change the texture of the food. You can also dehydrate fruits and veggies with the smoke, adding an additional layer of flavor. Smoke-dried tomatoes and jalapeños (chipotle peppers) are favorites.

- **Dehydrating and smoking jerky** is also done at lower temperatures and in drier conditions. This is where you can do away with most water pans. The smoke will not only dry the food, but the natural chemical reactions with the surface of the food also help cure the meat. This, along with the absence of moisture, makes the food inhospitable to dangerous bacteria and therefore acts as a preservative.

- Most **low-and-slow meat smoking** takes place between 225°F and 275°F. But just because you are cooking at lower temperatures doesn't mean you can't overcook your food. Different foods have different internal temperature targets. Leaner cuts of meat dry out easily (which is only acceptable for jerky).

- Some models allow for higher temperatures and this is best described as **smoke roasting**. Most of the baking and cooking you can do in your home oven you can also do in these types of smokers. The popular electric smokers mentioned in this book, however, are typically limited to around 275°F.

And, as with oven cooking, remember that simply opening the cook chamber door can dramatically slow cook times by quickly lowering the smoker's temperature.

Note: After two hours of direct smoke, many people believe that most of the smoke flavor has been absorbed by the meat. The heat from the oven element can carry the rest of the cooking to completion with or without additional smoke. In theory, if it rains, you can finish the rest of the cook time in your oven with success and still retain the great smoke flavor from the first couple of hours of direct smoke in the smoker.

OPTIONAL GEAR

The beautiful thing about electric smokers is that the cooker does most of the heavy lifting. Still, you'll want a few extra tools to get the job done. These help ensure properly cooked foods, ease transport to and from the smoker, lend a hand with cleanup and meal prep, and can boost your smokin' reputation (as with the cool cedar planks). The following are not mandatory, but at the very least they are super cool to have in your arsenal.

Thermometers

Thermometers are a must for the serious smoker. Even if your electric smoker comes with an internal thermometer, you'll probably want a more accurate digital "instant-read" thermometer. The internal temperature of your meat should be within the safe range according to the USDA's (usda.gov) food-safety standards (and hit more-demanding pit-master standards). ThermoWorks makes a popular waterproof thermometer called the Thermapen that sells for around $90, but there are newer, much more affordable options available, including Bluetooth thermometers that promise to wake you from your nap (via your smartphone) when the Boston butt hits the perfect internal temperature.

Electric Knives

Electric knives can slice brisket to the desired pencil-thin thickness.

Bear "Claws"

Bear "claws" are handheld pronged forks used to "pull" apart whole pork roasts for authentic pulled pork.

Frogmats

Frogmats—which are nonstick, heat-resistant mesh grill mats—prevent foods sticking to your grill grates and help make cleanup easier. They are dishwasher safe. Retail price is about $15.

Cast Iron Skillet

A small cast iron skillet always comes in handy for taking foods from smoker to stove top.

Cedar or Other Hardwood Planks

Cedar or other hardwood planks add flavor to smoked entrées, and you look uber cool serving your smoked salmon right on a smoking board!

Bisquette Savers

Aluminum Bradley Bisquette savers keep you from wasting expensive wood Bisquettes when you want to slow the feeding of wood disks. They run three for less than 20 bucks.

Digital Thermometer

Electric Knife

Bear "Claws"

Frogmats

Cast Iron Skillet

Hardwood Planks

Bisquette Savers

SAFETY, TROUBLE-SHOOTING, AND MAINTENANCE

I believe the quality electric smokers discussed in this book are the safest way to play with fire. You control the actual "live" fire as much as possible without extinguishing the wood. As with all equipment, it's important to take precautions, adapt when problems arise, and properly care for your electric smoker.

SAFETY BASICS

It's essential to remember that cooking equipment is the leading cause of house fires, according to the National Fire Protection Association. The old saying, "Where there's smoke, there's fire," is a bit misleading with the smolder machines, but you still need to use your head and watch out for a few dangers when cooking with an electric smoker.

The biggest danger is carbon monoxide gas. The owner manuals for all these electric smokers boldly warn of this gas danger: **Never use an electric smoker in an enclosed area.** Inside the house is clearly a bad idea to use a smoker, but enclosed porches and tents are less obviously dangerous.

To stay safe (and able to enjoy your delicious smoker results), keep the following safety tips in mind at all times.

- Don't allow woodchip ashes or spent Bisquettes to accumulate inside the smoker.

- Never operate your electric smoker in the rain. You wouldn't use a hair dryer in the tub, right?

- Avoid extension cords.

- Carefully dispose of wood ashes. Soak ashes with water and enclose them in an aluminum-foil pouch before discarding.

- Have a dedicated pit-master's fire extinguisher for your grill area (as well as another in the kitchen).

- Keep kids, pets, and vinyl siding a safe distance away from your cooker for the entire cooking process.

- Don't smoke with strange wood, particularly any scrap wood. Construction wood can be treated with poisonous chemicals and other undesirable materials.

- Be aware that electric smoker manufacturers do not want you to leave these cookers on for hours fully unattended. They express this in the fine-print warnings in the owner manuals, and in sales photos they keep it safe with the cook—still in eyeshot across the yard—in a hammock or in the home with the cooker in view from the window.

Accidents and cooking issues arise all the time. The most common problems occur with the accumulation of wood pucks, Bisquettes, or woodchips inside the cooking chamber. For a Bradley smoker, the pucks each burn for 20 minutes. So, to avoid the risk of fire, you need to empty the bowl of spent wood every two hours.

There is abundant evidence online of fires occurring inside almost all smokers. But you can relax a bit, knowing the fire dangers during both long and short cooks are greatly reduced with electric smokers. Again, remember that even the manufacturers don't want you to leave the cookers unattended. Avoid long smokes on uncovered wood decks or find a reputable fire-retardant mat to create a barrier over your wooden decking. A mat will actually also do a great job preventing grease stains from any drippings.

Finally, set up your electric smoker on a flat, stable surface. Most units have adjustable feet to help stabilize the base. Get in the habit of checking for wobbles before every use. The smoker door should remain open without you having to hold it open. And remember—despite the fact that some of these electric smokers feature handles and wheels—*you never want to move a hot smoker*.

BE PREPARED

Yes, things can go wrong, but being prepared can help keep you safe and safely smoking. Bear the following in mind to avoid potential barbecue disasters.

- Power issues are the most common problem for electric smokers. You need a dependable power source that won't trip circuit breakers.

- Grease fires are uncommon but have been reported when woodchips or pucks overflow or are exposed to air (uncovered). Keep proper fire-extinguishing equipment nearby, just in case.

- Woodchips can burn out and need to be replenished. Your smoker will continue to cook, just without the smoke flavor.

- Avoid using aluminum foil to wrap rack shelving, as doing so often restricts proper air and smoke flow.

- Over the extended life of your smoker, the heating element may die. Some are replaceable with factory parts.

- Clean the drip pans after each use. Many pit masters line the pans with aluminum foil to ease cleanup.

- Never use worn or damaged extension cords or run cords through water or snow.

- Never share extension cords or outlet power with multiple devices.

MAINTENANCE TIPS

Most electric smokers are beautifully simple to maintain. A few points to follow:

- **Keep it clean** by following each cook with a thorough wipe down, and remove all racks and pans to clean them.

- **Use a cover** while storing your smoker to prohibit nesting insects and also to block harsh sunlight that can deteriorate digital interfaces and buttons.

- **Unplug the smoker** when not in use for long periods of time.

TWO

WHAT TO FEED YOUR SMOKE

Because of the long history of roasting over wood, there is an almost infinite number of flavor combinations with which to experiment. Flavors can instantly and powerfully take the mind back to places in time—remember the food critic Anton Ego's flashback when eating the titular dish in Disney's *Ratatouille*? The infusion of smoke in myriad variations can move people on a very primitive level.

But will a food smoke? Some stars of the electric smoker are obvious, such as roasts and cheeses, but there are surprises, too. Cabbage? Mac and cheese? Bologna?

Here is a comprehensive chart listing the most popular smoking proteins and vegetables, many of which are used in this book, as well as some items you might not have thought of smoking but may want to try (just to impress yourself—or your neighbors and guests!).

Note: When it comes to smoking—especially barbecue favorites like pulled pork and brisket—"done" may not be to pit-master recommendations. The USDA recommends a "done" internal

Item to Smoke	Smoking Temp	Smoking Time	Internal Temp	Type of Woodchips
BEEF BRISKET	225°F	1½ hours per pound	190°F	OAK
BEEF JERKY	180°F	3 to 4 hours	To taste	HICKORY
BEEF SHORT RIBS	225°F	3 to 4 hours	175°F	MESQUITE, OAK
BOLOGNA	250°F	1 hour	To taste	HICKORY
CHUCK ROAST	225°F	1 hour per pound	145°F	MESQUITE, OAK
HAMBURGERS	225°F	1 hour	160°F	OAK
MEAT LOAF	225°F	2 hours	165°F	OAK
RIB EYE STEAK and PRIME RIB	225°F	30 to 40 minutes per pound	145°F	OAK
TRI-TIP STEAK	225°F	2 to 3 hours	145°F	RED OAK
BABY BACK RIBS	225°F	4 to 6 hours	190°F	HICKORY
BACON or CANDIED BACON	225°F	30 to 45 minutes	140°F	APPLEWOOD
GROUND PORK SAUSAGE 1 to 2 pounds	225°F	2 hours	165°F	APPLEWOOD
PORK SHOULDER Boston Butt	200°F	1½ hours per pound	205°F	HICKORY
PORK TENDERLOIN 8 to 10 pounds	225°F	4 to 6 hours	160°F	HICKORY
PRECOOKED HAM 5 to 7 pounds	275°F	5 hours	160°F	CHERRY
RACK OF LAMB	200°F	1¼ hours	145°F	APPLEWOOD, CHERRY, LILAC, OAK

CUTS OF BEEF AND PORK

BEEF

1. Neck
2. Chuck
3. Rib
4. Short Loin
5. Sirloin
6. Tenderloin
7. Top Sirloin
8. Rump Cap
9. Round
10. Brisket
11. Shank
12. Short Plate
13. Flank

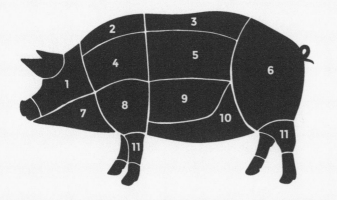

PORK

1. Head
2. Clear Plate
3. Back Fat
4. Boston Shoulder
5. Loin
6. Leg
7. Cheek
8. Picnic
9. Ribs
10. Bacon
11. Hock

Item to Smoke	Smoking Temp	Smoking Time	Internal Temp	Type of Woodchips
CRAB	200°F	15 minutes per pound	To taste	OAK
FISH	175°F to 225°F	2½ to 3 hours	145°F	ALDER, APPLEWOOD, CHERRY, OAK
LOBSTER	225°F	45 minutes	130°F to 140°F	ALDER, OAK
OYSTERS	225°F	1½ to 2 hours	To taste	APPLEWOOD, CHERRY, OAK
SALMON	200°F to 250°F	1 to 2 hours	145°F	ALDER, CEDAR PLANK
SCALLOPS	200°F	1 hour per pound	To taste	CHERRY, OAK
SHRIMP	175°F to 200°F	10 to 15 minutes per pound	Until pink	MESQUITE, PECAN
TUNA STEAKS	250°F	1 hour	145°F	APPLE, CHERRY, OAK
CHICKEN HALVES	250°F	3 hours	165°F	CHERRY
CHICKEN, PIECES Legs/Thighs/ Breasts/Wings	250°F	1½ to 2 hours	165°F	APPLEWOOD, CHERRY, OAK, PECAN
CHICKEN, WHOLE	250°F	3 to 4 hours (based on size)	165°F	APPLEWOOD, CHERRY, OAK, PECAN
GROUND CHICKEN or TURKEY	275°F	1 to 1½ hours	165°F	APPLEWOOD
HARDBOILED EGGS	200°F	20 to 30 minutes	To taste	HICKORY
JERK CHICKEN LEG QUARTERS	275°F	1½ hours	165°F	MESQUITE plus a few whole allspice berries

Item to Smoke	Smoking Temp	Smoking Time	Internal Temp	Type of Woodchips
TURKEY	250°F	30 minutes per pound	165°F	APPLEWOOD
TURKEY LEGS	225°F	4 to 6 hours	165°F	APPLEWOOD
QUAIL	225°F	1 hour	145°F	OLIVE
ARTICHOKES	225°F	2 hours	Until done	MAPLE
ASPARAGUS	240°F	1 hour	Until done	MAPLE
BELL PEPPERS	225°F	1½ hours	Until done	MAPLE
CABBAGE	240°F	2 hours	Until done	APPLEWOOD, MAPLE, OAK
CAULIFLOWER	200°F to 250°F	45 minutes to 1½ hours	Until tender	MAPLE
CORN ON THE COB	225°F	1½ to 2 hours	Until done	MAPLE
EGGPLANT	200°F	1 to 1½ hours	Until done	MAPLE
GARLIC	225°F	2 hours	Until done	OAK
JALAPEÑO PEPPERS	250°F	1 to 1½ hours	To taste	MAPLE
MUSHROOMS	225°F	1½ hours	Until done	OAK
ONIONS	225°F to 255°F	2 hours	Until done	MAPLE, MESQUITE, HICKORY
PEACHES	200°F	35 to 45 minutes	Until done	MAPLE
PINEAPPLE	250°F	1 to 1½ hours	Until done	MAPLE

Item to Smoke	Smoking Temp	Smoking Time	Internal Temp	Type of Woodchips
POTATOES, SWEET POTATOES	225°F to 250°F	2 to 2½ hours	Until done	MAPLE, PECAN
SQUASH, ZUCCHINI	225°F	1 hour	Until done	MAPLE
TOMATOES	200°F	45 minutes	Until done	OAK
DUCK, WHOLE 4 to 5 pounds	225°F	3 to 3½ hours	165°F	CHERRY, PECAN
CORNISH GAME HENS	275°F	2 to 3 hours	170°F	APPLEWOOD, OLIVE
ALLIGATOR	225°F	2 hours	165°F	MESQUITE
VENISON	225°F	1 hour per pound	160°F	HICKORY
CHEESES	Under 90°F	30 to 45 minutes	To taste	HICKORY, MESQUITE
MAC AND CHEESE	225°F	1 hour	Until bubbly	HICKORY, MESQUITE
NUTS	225°F	1 hour	To taste	HICKORY, MESQUITE
SNACK MIX	225°F	2 to 2½ hours	Until dry	HICKORY, MESQUITE

temperature for food-safety reasons—but to get to fall-off-the-bone or succulent pull-apart texture (for a Boston butt) you need to *far* exceed USDA recommendations.

With slow-smoked barbecue, "done" can be witnessed by that fall-apart, yet juicy texture. The collagen and intramuscular fat break down and render deliciously into the meat. The smoke ring—although a badge of honor—is not necessarily a sign of "done" by pit-master standards. Best to use an instant-read thermometer to be sure you've hit your target temperature.

FLAVORS OF WOOD

My first question when determining the credibility of a new barbecue joint is, "Can you smell the smoke from the parking lot?" Next question

THE ART & SCIENCE OF ELECTRIC SMOKING

Creating something as spectacular as pulled pork is beautifully simple with an electric smoker—but it won't be quick. Planning is key. Here are the steps:

1 The night before you cook (let's call this "Smokin' Eve"), season the pork roast with a good rub and refrigerate it overnight.

2 The next day, start clean. Unless you want your first meal to have that new-car smell, it is a standard best practice across all lines of electric smokers to do a first burn in a new smoker for an hour to "season" it by burning off any impurities in the machine. Even if the cooker is not straight out of the box, it is a good idea (and my common practice) to clean the cooker, dispose of any accumulated grease, oil, or wood debris, and "fire it up" on the highest setting for a few minutes.

3 Prep the food. A large cut of meat, such as a Boston butt, takes time to come to room temperature after a night in the refrigerator. Place the meat in the smoker and let it come fully off its chill and up to cooking temperature in the smoker. This will cause a drop in the smoker's temperature, but it's considered safer than leaving the meat out to come to room temperature over a long period of time.

4 Place the temperature probe into the center of the thickest part of the meat.

5 Wash your hands for food-safety reasons and the clean operation of the machinery.

6 Fill the water pan with warm water and put it in place.

7 Adjust the controls until the cooker maintains a steady and stable cooking temperature.

8 Begin feeding the cooker with wood and replenish it every 30 minutes, or when you see smoke production diminish. You want the smolder to go slowly. At the lowest temperatures, the wood releases carbon dioxide, which, when combined with the charred wood, creates carbon monoxide and nitrogen dioxide. The fumes condense and dissolve on the surface of the meat where they diffuse into the meat to slowly create that iconic reddish smoke ring.

9 Repeat but resist. Feed with wood as needed, but resist opening the cooker's door more than absolutely needed—resist the urge to peek. You want to keep a constant temperature inside.

10 When the meat reaches an internal temperature of 165°F, remember that the meat is *not* done—despite USDA recommendations! You may opt to wrap, mop, or spritz hourly. Wood and smoke are now secondary, as the meat will have absorbed most of the wood's flavor.

11 Once the meat hits an internal temperature of 190°F, remove it and wrap it with the "Texas Crutch"— aluminum foil—and include a cup or two of your favorite liquid. Then let the meat rest for an hour before pulling.

is, "What kind of wood do they use?" Sometimes it seems like our number of wood choices can be overwhelming, but the choice is almost as important as the decision to smoke your food in the first place. The decision can be a bit like picking out a barbecue sauce at the supermarket. I freeze with the number of options!

The reality is that in the United States the most popular woods (popular, not *poplar*) to smoke with are oak and hickory. But I encourage you to expand your horizons and experiment with different flavors. I live in the Lowcountry of South Carolina where pecan is plentiful, so it's a great choice. Hickory is used a lot in competition barbecue, so the smell of hickory in the air always takes me back to an early-Saturday-morning competition. Applewood brings to mind a relaxing Cracker Barrel breakfast (maybe it's their bacon?). Whichever wood you choose, it can take your brain, nose, and taste buds back to special times. There's just something primitive about how the brain connects with smoke flavors. I think it's been baked into our DNA for centuries.

Experiment, but choose wisely. Everything's available on the Internet these days. Look for an updated list of recommended vendors on my resources page at *BarbecueTricks*.

To help you decide, here is a handy guide to the woods used in this book.

Apple   Hickory   Oak

Wood	Smoke Flavor	What to Cook With
APPLE	Slightly sweet but dense and fruity	Beef, poultry, game birds, pork, ham
APRICOT	Milder and sweeter than hickory	Most meats
ASH	Fast burning; light but distinctive	Fish and red meats
CHERRY	Slightly sweet and fruity	All meats
HICKORY	Pungent, smoky, bacon-like; the most common wood used (especially in the South)	All smoking, especially pork and ribs
MAPLE	Mild and somewhat sweet	Pork, poultry, cheese, vegetables, and small game birds
MESQUITE	Strong and earthy; most popular grilling wood in Texas	Most meats, especially beef, and most vegetables
OAK	Heavy; the second-most popular wood. Many pit masters consider red oak to be the best.	Red meat, pork, fish, and heavy game
PEACH	Woodsy and slightly sweet	Most meats
PECAN	More like oak than hickory, but not as strong	Most meats
ACACIA	Mesquite family; strong	Most meats, beef, vegetables
ALDER	Delicate with a hint of sweetness	Fish, pork, poultry, light game birds, and especially great with salmon
ALMOND	Nutty and sweet, light ash	All meats
BIRCH	Maple-like; medium-hard wood	Great choice for pork and poultry
CAMPHOR	Exotic wood used in China; strong distinct flavor	Typically duck

Wood	Smoke Flavor	What to Cook With
CEDAR	Used for plank cooking; try shingles, too	Typically salmon
COTTON-WOOD	Mild	Most meats
GRAPEFRUIT	Slightly fruity; medium smoke	Excellent with beef, pork, poultry
GRAPEVINE	Aromatic, similar to fruitwoods	All meats
LEMON	Slightly fruity; medium smoke	Excellent with beef, pork, poultry
LILAC	Very light, subtle, with a hint of floral	Seafood, lamb
MULBERRY	Sweet smell reminiscent of apple	Beef, poultry, game birds, pork, ham
NECTARINE	Milder and sweeter than hickory	Most meats
ORANGE	Slightly fruity; medium smoke	Excellent with beef, pork, poultry
PEAR	Slightly sweet, woodsy	Poultry, game birds, pork
PIMENTO	The wood of allspice (pimento berry), spicy, similar to mesquite	The best choice for jerk chicken
PLUM	Milder and sweeter than hickory	Most meats
TEA LEAVES	Tea; Chinese method	Duck, white meats, fish
WALNUT	Very heavy smoke: usually mixed with a lighter wood such as pecan or apple; can be bitter if used alone or not aged	Red meats, game
WHISKEY BARREL	Aged oak from Jack Daniel's whiskey	Most meats

YOUR SMOKING PANTRY

When it comes to heirloom-quality barbecue recipes, often it's the method and cook time that create the "secret." There are just a handful of ingredients that can be considered "pantry essentials" for barbecue. Two must-haves: herbs and spices. What's the difference?

- Herbs grow. They're leafy (not woody) and, in cooking, they don't really like heat. Add herbs at the end of the cook time.

- Spices like heat. Typically, spices come from bark, seeds, roots, and buds.

PANTRY ESSENTIALS

- **Allspice (pimento berry):** the key to jerk seasoning.

- **Bouillon cubes:** Concentrated beef (or chicken) blocks add a blast of flavor when tucked inside a roasted onion.

- **Cajun seasoning**

- **Cayenne pepper**

- **Celery salt and celery seed:** The distinct flavor of celery seeds adds a natural punch of smoke ring–enhancing natural nitrite. Keep both celery salt (a must for a Chicago hot dog) and celery seed (grind it yourself) handy and use the best option to control the saltiness of your rubs.

- **Chili powder:** Make your own for the best flavor.

- **Coffee:** The new micro-ground instant coffees are great in rubs.

- **Coriander, (cilantro seed)** ground: Rendezvous, a rib restaurant in Memphis, Tennessee, turned me on to this mind-blowing flavor.

- **Cumin,** ground

- **Garlic powder**

- **Ginger,** ground

- **Mustard,** dry

- **Onion,** fresh and dried: The secret to fast food's famous "special sauce" and little square hamburger sliders.

- **Paprika,** sweet and smoked

- **Peppercorns,** always grind to order

- **Red pepper flakes:** A little bit goes a long way, but they kick up flavor.

- **Salt,** kosher: The coarse grains of a name-brand kosher salt allow for better control in recipes and rubs.

- **Salt:** Morton's Tender Quick, a.k.a. Fab, is a curing salt that enhances the smoke ring.

- **Sugar,** turbinado: See sidebar page 24.

- **Tamarind concentrate**

NOT ALL SUGAR IS CREATED EQUAL

It is worth noting that all sugar is not created equal. In smoking barbecue-rub and sauce recipes, white refined sugar is often replaced with brown sugar as it adds a deeper flavor. Pit masters prefer turbinado sugar (Sugar In The Raw is a good brand) because it is a less-processed form of crystalized sugar that stands up to heat. Plus, its larger crystals add a welcome texture to robust rubs.

Sugars and sweet sauces are normally added at the very end of high-heat grilling, but the low-and-slow temperatures in your electric smoker shouldn't get high enough to burn them. Use caution if your smoker can get hotter than most. The burning point (scorch point) of sugar is just above 330°F.

What? You want to make a sauce for the incredible brisket you just smoked? Let's agree to serve it on the side, okay? Here are a few shelf staples for sauces.

- **Ketchup:** Watch your sweetness and sugar quantity.

- **Mustard:** Cheap, yellow, and generic. It's often used as a simple precook adherent for rubs.

- **Vinegar:** Apple cider vinegar is the main punch in most sauces, especially in North Carolina.

- **Worcestershire sauce:** Use the good stuff. Fun fact: The secret punch behind its bold flavor is anchovies.

SMOKING IN BULK

The beauty of the new electric smokers is that there is plenty of space to smoke more than just a meal. The top-of-the-line 40-inch Masterbuilt boasts 975 square inches of cabinet space. Char-Broil offers a 1,000-square-inch version with a large-capacity smoke tray for chips to burn for up to seven hours before reloading.

Slabs of ribs can occupy a lot of shelf space. If you want to smoke ribs in bulk, invest in rib hooks to hang the slabs vertically in the smoker. Also make sure to leave 1 to 2 inches of space between the pieces to allow for good air and smoke flow around each piece of meat.

If you are a hunter, maximize your smoking space by grinding the meat into sausage casings for cured and smoked sausages in bulk. These can also be hung from the ceiling of the smoker to maximize space and allow for the best air and smoke flow. The sausages also freeze well.

If you compete in barbecue contests and are able to use electric power (some sanctioning organizations do not allow electric smokers), maximize your cooking space and give yourself an edge by cooking multiple entries and submitting only the best and most beautiful results. Instead of just two racks, cook four and select the best. Dark-meat chicken thighs are inexpensive but hold up well to long cook times by retaining moisture. Cook double the amount and cherry-pick the best for turn-in. **Here's a tip:** Many competitors who cook chicken remove the skin from the chicken thighs and shave and scrape off any excess fat before replacing the skin and smoking the chicken. This creates that coveted "bite through" skin.

Cooking for school lunches? Drumsticks are hard to beat for kid-appeal and for price. Smoked cheeses, smoked nut mixes, turkey breasts, beef sticks, and beef jerky can be convenient choices for knocking out a month of brown-bag meals and snacks. Portable protein packs are popular in school lunches today. Providing a variety of nuts, cheese, and meat will give kids a satisfying amount of protein to keep them full and focused into the afternoon.

STOCKPILING SMOKED FOODS

For centuries, smokehouses were used to preserve and prolong the freshness of meats and stave off bacteria and spoilage. These days our preparation conditions are cleaner and we often work with curing salts (another great bacteria inhibitor). But the long exposure to smoke actually builds an acidic coating around the meat that deters bacteria growth. The process becomes similar to a cure by also dehydrating the surface (and below it) of the meat, making it more difficult for potentially harmful bacteria to survive.

Even though we now have modern refrigeration and freezing for long-term storage, there are still a few things to consider when stockpiling smoked goodies, as each type of meat has different characteristics.

Brisket can be refrigerated and reheated, and is often *better* the next day. However, you need to know that the rich outer skin, or "bark," loses its succulent crispness after refrigeration and freezing. You also need to be careful not to dry out the beef when you reheat it. You can safely freeze beef for 4 to 12 months.

Pork butt is similar to a whole brisket when it comes to freezing. The bark will also lose its mojo, but the internal fat will help keep the end product moist. It is better to leave the roast whole, instead of pulling or chopping the meat because small pieces tend to get freezer burn easily. Ideally, freeze pork butt in portion sizes you can consume in one meal. The full roast should freeze safely for 4 to 12 months.

Cooked spare ribs and baby backs lose the best qualities of bark and a lot of texture, so avoid freezing. If you do freeze these cuts, they will remain safe to eat for 3 to 9 months.

Chicken is better to freeze whole. Refrigeration can enhance the smoke flavor, but the skin can get rubbery. Freeze whole chicken or turkey for up to 1 year, and smaller pieces for up to 9 months.

Fresh fish is best stored frozen in water, but once smoked, freeze it in vacuum-sealed containers within 12 hours of being smoked. In cold storage it should keep for 3 to 6 months. Refreezing a second time is not recommended.

Smoke, curing salt, and storage techniques help preserve flavor. Here are a few tricks to consider:

- Keep your freezer at a low and consistent temperature of 0°F. This is the optimal temperature to avoid freezer burn, providing your meat is well wrapped.

- Seal the meat in airtight wrapping. Many hunters who store in bulk use a vacuum-sealing machine like the FoodSaver to master the wrapping.

- Put a second wrapping of aluminum foil over your original airtight seal of plastic wrap. Most plastic wrap tends to lose its cling when cold. An extra layer and seal of foil will keep it tight.

- If you are storing large amounts of summer sausage, start with an exceptionally sterile environment and a recipe that includes a good curing salt. Some hunters also suggest soaking the sausage casings in apple cider vinegar before stuffing, to reduce bacteria and mold issues in storage.

When it comes to thawing frozen smoked meats, use as much thought and care as you did when preparing them for storage. Don't just leave the food out on the counter until it comes to room temperature. The USDA suggests the tried-and-true method of transferring the frozen food to the refrigerator and letting it slowly thaw. This will take time but has the added benefit of you being able to refreeze the meat before, and even after, a complete thaw if your plans change.

If you plan to cook the meat immediately, speed the process by giving the wrapped meat a cold-water bath, circulating and exchanging cool tap water into the bath. Bear in mind that with this method, there is no refreezing allowed.

COOKOUTS

The thrill of the grill is nothing compared to the pride of the pit master when revealing his feast for a large gathering of friends. You will be the rock star at the next cookout, tailgate, or holiday feast, and your friends will be laying premium craft beer at your feet so that you'll keep inviting them back.

With good planning and plenty of time you can actually cook several recipes at once. Below are some proven tips to keep things under control.

- Create a good timeline that includes you revealing the impressively large cut of meat as your guests arrive.

- Use your smoker shelves in stages and back-time each recipe just as you would plan oven time for Thanksgiving dinner. Main meat loads first. Appetizers and quicker-cooking veggies can be loaded last, and will hold until serving.

· Consider which foods will drip onto which other foods. Some drippings add great flavor, others not so much.

· Allow for extra cook time when adding cold food to food already cooking in the smoker.

· Use the lower racks of your smoker (closer to the heating element) for food items that are more resilient to higher heat, or plan to rotate your racks if needed.

· Allow for good smoke flow around all your food items by leaving 1 to 2 inches of space around each piece.

· Rib slabs and sausage links may fit better when hanging from the smoker's ceiling on meat hooks. Even if you don't actually need to hang the ribs, you'll look extra cool if you do.

COOKOUT MENUS

Any Old Day

· Smoked Tri-Tip Roast (page 76) with Java Rub (page 171)

· Cajun Shrimp (page 107)

· Smoked Onion Bombs (page 133)

· Baba Ghanouj (page 124)

· Beer: Stout

Family Reunion

· Jamaican Jerk Chicken (page 46)

· Competition Baby Back Ribs (page 58)

· Armadillo "Eggs" (page 126)

· Potato Bacon Bites (page 143)

· Beer: Lager

Easter Brunch

· Rack of Lamb (page 123) with Chimichurri Sauce (page 169)

· Holiday Ham (page 71) with Pineapple–Brown Sugar Sauce (page 168)

· Loaded Hasselback Potatoes (page 135)

· Smoked Deviled Eggs (page 141)

· Pair with Bourbon

· Beer: Pale Ale

Spring Picnic

· Unbelievably Moist Brisket (page 79)

· Plum Chicken Pops (page 50) with Plum Sauce (page 172)

· Smoked Corn on the Cob (page 142)

· Smoked Bacon-Wrapped Onion Rings (page 138)

· Pair with Tennessee Whiskey

· Beer: American Porter

July 4th Backyard Barbecue

- Slow-Smoked Ancho Chile–Rubbed Boston Butt (Pulled Pork; page 59) with Spicy Hickory-Smoked Barbecue Sauce (page 163)

- Smoked Italian Sausage (page 69)

- Smoked Mac and Cheese (page 149)

- Smoked Coleslaw (page 131)

- Pair with Tennessee Whiskey

- Beer: Pale Ale

WHAT ARE WE DRINKING?

With the smoking done, it's time to toast the hard work and lip-smacking flavors of your feast. Great barbecue has characteristics akin to great whiskey—smoky flavors born out of hardwood, charcoal, and slow-aging. I recently toured the Jack Daniel's distillery in Tennessee. There you can see firsthand how fire, smoke, charcoal, and time combine to create something very special. In just one step of the elaborate process they create a massive fire right inside the distillery grounds in Lynchburg. Three days a week the crew ignites massive pallets of hard sugar maple into a fiery blaze simply to create the purest black mellowing charcoal. *Wood, fire, and time.* It's no surprise that the rich flavors of dark whiskey pair well with smoked foods.

If you go to fancy food festivals you may hear of "bubble-cue" events—with bubbly champagne cited as a perfect smoked food pairing because of its bubbles. But I think even champagne mixed with ripple ("champipple" as Fred Sanford called it) is still a bit too pretentious. In my humble opinion, beer is the other great match for barbecue and smoked delicacies. The bubbly effervescence cuts through the rich, fatty, salty succulence to delightfully wash down every smoky bite.

Think beer and whiskey are too unpretentious for your slow-smoked delicacies? Think beyond the six-pack:

- Got a perfect slab of hickory-smoked ribs? Try a woody bourbon aged for 2 to 8 years in oak barrels.

- Pulled pork pairs nicely with a Tennessee whiskey, with its hint of charcoal, in cola or in a Lynchburg Lemonade. In the world of beer, pulled pork also pairs perfectly with a hoppier brew such as a pale ale that cuts through spicy seasonings.

- Beefy steaks are a perfect match for the smokiness of a Scotch, aged 3 to 30 years.

- Slow-roasted and smoked wings pair nicely with a rich porter that complements their heavier smoky flavor.

- Chicken and pork cuts with lighter seasoning go well with a classic pilsner.

- Heartier briskets and meats with bold sauces will withstand a heavy-duty brew such as a dark lager, an IPA, or a brown ale. Match strength with strength.

- If you're keeping it light with smoked veggies and seafood, try a pilsner.

- Whiskey and smoked cheeses make a spectacular first course. The general rule is to pair a harder cheese with a lighter whiskey and a creamier cheese with a heavier whiskey.

- If you have spicy meat, such as Jamaican Jerk Chicken (page 46), opt for an amber ale or a pale lager such as Red Stripe.

- The smoked salmon you can master with your electric smoker is often paired with champagne, but I think it's even better with a malt whiskey or a weissbier (wheat beer).

- You can't go wrong pairing sausage with almost any beer. If you want a classic match, look for a great German lager.

2

LET'S SMOKE SOME MEAT

Sweet Sriracha Barbecue Chicken, page 44

THREE

POULTRY

36 Smoked Beer-Can Chicken

37 Herb-Smoked Quail

38 Crispy-Skin
    Orange Chicken

39 Buffalo Chicken Balls

40 Garlic-Herb Turkey Legs

41 Chipotle Wings

42 Drunken Drumsticks

44 Sweet Sriracha
    Barbecue Chicken

45 Applewood-Smoked
    Turkey Breast

46 Jamaican Jerk Chicken

47 Cinnamon-Cured
    Fire-Smoked Chicken

48 Smoky Brined Turkey

49 Caramelized Honey
    Buffalo Chicken

50 Plum Chicken Pops

51 Mesquite Maple-
    Bacon Chicken

Electric smokers are coveted chicken cookers. Slow-roasting and smoke takes the simple bird to another level, absorbing and highlighting all the subtle sweetness in the meat and also the unique flavors in hardwood and fruitwood smoke.

Your electric smoker will do the perfect job on chicken and turkey with this simple formula: *Smoke at 250°F for 40 minutes per pound until the internal temperature hits 165°F in the thickest part of the meat.* Easy.

The trick to smoking chicken and turkey is to allow the fatty skin to render out, which keeps it from being chewy.

A savory infusion of hickory smoke can take a boring baked chicken and turn it into a pit-master's masterpiece—so flavorful you won't want to add sauce!

CUTS

You can't go wrong with chicken. All cuts have a home in your electric smoker.

- **Breast meat** is the most delicate in the poultry world. Lean and clean, the breast is a first choice for some. However, the breast is also the easiest cut to dry out and is typically more expensive.

- **Thighs** are a pit-master's choice because they are resistant to drying out. They are difficult to overcook and offer plenty of succulent (read: fatty) skin to delight your inner fat kid.

- **Legs** or **drumsticks** are also top choices for cookouts and kids. You gotta love when Mother Nature offers you food on a stick.

- **Wings** have been upgraded from a cheap cut to a tailgate delicacy these days. Separate whole wings into wingettes and drumettes when feeding a crowd.

- There is always the **whole bird**. Take care not to overcook the breast before the thighs are cooked, but there's nothing quite as spectacular as a whole golden-brown smoked turkey on the table.

TECHNIQUES

Simple techniques for prepping chicken and turkey for smoking include *injecting*, *brining*, *seasoning*, and *dry-brining*.

- When injecting the meat, insert the injector needle through the interior of the ribcage so you don't pierce and blemish the outer skin.

- For brining, use this ratio of salt to water: *1 gallon of water mixed with 1 cup of kosher salt*. Remember to keep the meat and brine chilled to prevent food contamination.

- When seasoning the whole bird, or its parts, I always season under the skin and into the muscles of all parts of the bird. It's a little extra effort but you'll get salt and real flavor into the meat. Poultry skin—especially thick turkey skin—is like a wetsuit. Nothing will get seasoned *through* the skin so you have to get *under* it.

- Dry-brining is something I use to enhance the creation of crispy skin. Rub the exterior and interior of the skin and meat with your favorite salt rub and refrigerate it uncovered for 4 hours. Blot the skin completely dry before smoking.

TURKEY TIP

Instead of going all out with a massive 20-pound turkey, opt for two 12-pound birds. You'll have double the drumsticks, double the smoky surface area, and will be able to dramatically cut your cook time. Face it: You usually have half a turkey left over anyway.

SPATCHCOCKING

One way to trim your poultry is with a "butterflied" technique called spatchcocking. To spatchcock a whole chicken, simply cut out the backbone and spread out both sides. Use a sharp knife or poultry shears (I like the shears that can be separated into two parts and washed in the dishwasher) to remove or split the small breast bone to allow both sides to spread out flat on the grate and give all sides full exposure to that delicious smoke.

CLEANING

Do you need to wash your bird? These days, many barbecue gurus say it is not necessary and that having additional raw-poultry contact in your cleaning area increases the risk of bacterial contamination. That said, I always wash the exterior and interior of poultry before seasoning. This is also a great time to remove any packaged parts stuffed inside the cavity. If your turkey has one of those pop-up thermometers, you can leave it in, as your smoker's temperature will be lower than a typical oven's (if you're doing it right).

FINAL TIPS FOR POULTRY BARBECUE SUCCESS

In addition to what you've just learned, the following can help your poultry be its best barbecue self:

- Watch supermarket labeling for terms like "enhanced." Think of this as prebrined with salty broth. Track this to control the amount of salt in your recipes.

- Poultry can transmit food-borne illnesses. Wash your hands often when preparing poultry and keep raw poultry separate from smoked.

- As noted in the Techniques section, poultry skin is like a wetsuit. Dry seasonings need to be rubbed over *and* under the skin—or applied via marinade or brine.

- Always marinate poultry in the refrigerator (and do not reuse marinades).

- You can't judge a book by its cover: Always use a thermometer to ensure poultry is thoroughly cooked.

Whatever you call this—Beer Butt Chicken, Beer in the Rear, or simply Beer Can Chicken—this technique is best appreciated for keeping the meat moist. Just watch your balance.

SMOKED BEER-CAN CHICKEN

SERVES 3 OR 4 | **250°F** | **APPLE, CHERRY, OAK, OR PECAN**

PREP TIME: 30 minutes

SMOKE TIME: 3 to 4 hours

FOR THE INJECTION

½ cup (1 stick) melted butter

½ cup apple cider vinegar

¼ cup Cajun seasoning

1 teaspoon garlic powder

1 teaspoon onion powder

1 (3- to 4-pound) whole chicken

FOR THE RUB

Olive oil

¾ cup Cajun seasoning

1 (12-ounce) can beer

FOR THE MOP

1 cup apple cider

½ cup olive oil

TO MAKE THE INJECTION

1. In a small bowl, whisk together the butter, vinegar, Cajun seasoning, garlic powder, and onion powder.

2. Use a meat-injecting syringe to inject the liquid into various spots in the chicken. Inject about half the mixture into the breasts and the other half throughout the rest of the chicken.

TO MAKE THE RUB

1. Rub the chicken all over with olive oil and apply a generous layer of Cajun seasoning.

2. Drink or discard half the beer and place the beer can on a stable surface. Place the bird's cavity on top of the can and position the chicken so it will sit up by itself. Prop the legs forward to make it more stable, or buy a specially made stand to hold the beer can and chicken in place.

3. Preheat the smoker to about 250°F with the apple, cherry, oak, or pecan wood.

TO MAKE THE MOP

1. In a 12-ounce or larger spray bottle, combine the cider and olive oil. Cover and shake before each use.

2. Put the chicken in the smoker and spray it with the mop about every 30 minutes to keep it moist.

3. Smoke the chicken for 3 to 4 hours, or until the internal temperature of the thickest meat reaches 165°F.

PREPARATION TIP: Experiment by adding freshly cut aromatic herbs to the beer can, and try some drinks other than beer, such as fruity sodas.

Delicate fowl such as quail and small game birds are perfect for electric smokers. My father-in-law has years of experience hunting and preparing quail in and around the shooting clubs of South Carolina where they used a more rustic cooking method for lunch in the field.

He says the quail were broiled on a wire grate laid over the top of a charcoal bucket. These pots provided extreme direct heat. While cooking, the quail were basted with a mixture of oil, vinegar, salt, and pepper, which sizzled and smoked as the oil dripped onto the charcoal. When the quail were medium-rare to just short of well-done, the hungry hunters enjoyed a feast.

HERB-SMOKED QUAIL

SERVES 4 TO 6 | **225°F** | **HICKORY**

PREP TIME: 10 minutes
SMOKE TIME: 1 hour

4 to 6 quail
2 tablespoons olive oil
Salt
Freshly ground black pepper
1 package dry Hidden Valley Ranch Dressing Mix
½ cup (1 stick) butter, melted

1. Preheat the smoker to 225°F with the hickory wood.

2. Brush the quail with the olive oil and season with salt and pepper. Place the quail in the smoker and smoke for about 1 hour.

3. In a small bowl, stir together the ranch-dressing mix and melted butter.

4. Thirty minutes into the smoking process, brush the quail with the ranch-butter sauce and repeat at the end of the cook time. The quail are done when the internal temperature reaches 145°F.

SMOKING TIP: Load it up! You can smoke a bunch of quail and beautifully feed a crowd. Just be sure to allow for good air and smoke flow. Arrange the birds on the grill grate with 1 to 2 inches of space between each.

If you are a fan of dark meat, you will love this rich and sweet feast. A bonus: Leg quarters are probably the most affordable of all barbecue meats. Feed a crew on pennies and keep your inner cheapskate happy.

CRISPY-SKIN ORANGE CHICKEN

SERVES 4 | **275°F** | **APPLE**

MARINATING TIME: 8 hours
PREP TIME: 30 minutes
SMOKE TIME: 1½ to 2 hours

FOR THE POULTRY SPICE RUB

4 teaspoons paprika

1 tablespoon chili powder

2 teaspoons ground cumin

2 teaspoons dried thyme

2 teaspoons salt

2 teaspoons garlic powder

1 teaspoon freshly ground black pepper

FOR THE MARINADE

4 chicken quarters

2 cups frozen orange-juice concentrate

½ cup soy sauce

1 tablespoon garlic powder

TO MAKE THE SPICE RUB

In a small bowl, mix together the paprika, chili powder, cumin, thyme, salt, garlic powder, and pepper. Set aside.

TO MAKE THE MARINADE

1. Place the chicken quarters in a dish that will accommodate the marinade and chicken.

2. In a medium bowl, whisk the orange-juice concentrate (do not add water), soy sauce, garlic powder, and half the spice-rub mixture. Pour the marinade over the chicken, cover, and refrigerate for a minimum of 8 hours.

3. Preheat the smoker with the applewood to a stabilized 275°F.

4. Discard the marinade and rub all surfaces of the chicken generously with the remaining spice rub. Place the chicken quarters in the smoker for 1½ to 2 hours.

5. Remove the chicken from the smoker once a digital thermometer inserted in the breast has reached 160°F. Let it rest for 10 minutes, after which the temperature should have risen to 165°F.

PREPARATION TIP: Chicken thighs can have a lot of fatty skin, which you will want to trim. Promote that crispy bite through the skin by using a sharp knife to shave as much of the thick fat away from the underside of the skin, too.

All the spicy glory of buffalo wings without the bones. These meatballs also bake up to a tasty breaded nugget texture.

BUFFALO CHICKEN BALLS

MAKES 20 BALLS | **275°F** | **APPLE**

PREP TIME: 30 minutes
SMOKE TIME: 1 to 1½ hours

FOR THE BALLS

1 pound ground chicken

2 cups dry Bisquick mix

2 cups grated Cheddar cheese

¼ cup water

1 teaspoon chicken bouillon powder

1 (8-ounce) block blue cheese, cut into 20 cubes

FOR THE BUFFALO SAUCE

½ cup (1 stick) butter, melted

1 cup Frank's RedHot sauce

2 teaspoons cayenne pepper

1 teaspoon chopped fresh parsley leaves

Ranch dressing, for dipping

Preheat the smoker to 275°F with the applewood, which offers a light, sweet flavor contrasted with the spicy ingredients.

TO MAKE THE BALLS

1. In a medium bowl, mix together the chicken, Bisquick mix, Cheddar cheese, water, and bouillon powder. Take a cube of blue cheese, and form about 2 tablespoons (just enough to cover the cube) of the chicken mixture around the cube. Roll it into a ball. Repeat with the remaining cheese cubes and chicken mixture.

2. Place the balls on the smoker rack and smoke for 1 to 1½ hours until firm and the internal temperature reaches 160°F.

TO MAKE THE BUFFALO SAUCE

1. While the balls smoke, stir together the butter, hot sauce, and cayenne in a small bowl.

2. Dredge the cooked chicken balls in the hot sauce and sprinkle with the parsley before serving with ranch dressing.

PAIR IT: Serve these saucy buffalo chicken balls with a platter of crisp carrots, celery, and assorted smoked chilled veggies to dip.

There's something about eating a turkey leg that makes me want to wave it around in the air as I alternate barking out orders to my henchmen with indignation and taking big bites as the sauce drips down to my elbows. That's how I imagine being royalty. It's good to be king!

GARLIC-HERB TURKEY LEGS

SERVES 8 | **225°F** | **APPLE**

BRINING TIME: 4 hours
PREP TIME: 30 minutes
SMOKE TIME: 4 to 6 hours

FOR THE SPICE RUB

3 tablespoons onion powder

2 tablespoons paprika

1 tablespoon garlic powder

1 teaspoon freshly ground black pepper

1 teaspoon ground cumin

½ teaspoon dried rubbed sage

3 tablespoons vegetable oil or light olive oil

FOR THE BRINE

1 gallon water

1 cup kosher salt

½ cup sugar

2 tablespoons onion powder

1 tablespoon garlic powder

1 tablespoon chili powder

1 tablespoon paprika

1 tablespoon freshly ground black pepper

1 teaspoon dried rubbed sage

1 teaspoon ground cumin

8 turkey legs

TO MAKE THE SPICE RUB

In a small bowl, stir together the onion powder, paprika, garlic powder, pepper, cumin, sage, and vegetable oil. Set aside.

TO MAKE THE BRINE

1. In a container large enough to hold the brine and the turkey legs, combine the water with the salt, sugar, onion powder, garlic powder, chili powder, paprika, pepper, sage, and cumin, and stir until dissolved.

2. Place the turkey legs into the brine, cover, and refrigerate for a minimum of 4 hours.

3. Preheat the smoker to 225°F with the applewood.

4. Remove the legs, rinse them well, and discard the brine. Dry the drumsticks well with paper towels.

5. Coat the legs with the spice rub and place them into the smoker for 4 to 6 hours until the internal temperature reaches 165°F.

6. Remove the legs and let them rest for about 15 minutes before serving.

PREPARATION TIP: Use 1 cup of curing salt (such as Tender Quick) in your brine and soak for 12 to 24 hours to achieve the deep-pink color and hammy texture of the Disneyland version.

A chipotle pepper is not a type or variety of hot chile pepper but rather a way that jalapeño peppers are prepared. Jalapeños are smoked, dried, and typically packed wet in cans. Use their accompanying juice (adobo sauce) as a blazing-hot secret ingredient in everything from barbecue sauces to marinades.

CHIPOTLE WINGS

MAKES 45 TO 50 WINGS | **250°F** | **OAK**

MARINATING TIME: 1 hour
PREP TIME: 15 minutes
SMOKE TIME: 1½ to 2 hours

2 tablespoons packed light-brown sugar

1½ tablespoons chipotle peppers

1 tablespoon Hungarian smoked paprika

1 tablespoon dry mustard

1 tablespoon ground cumin

1½ teaspoons salt

5½ pounds chicken wings

1. In a small bowl, mix together the brown sugar, chipotles, paprika, mustard, cumin, and salt.

2. Place the chicken wings into a large resealable freezer bag and pour in the seasoning mix. Seal and shake the contents to coat the chicken generously. Refrigerate the wings for a minimum of 1 hour.

3. Preheat the smoker to 250°F with the oak wood.

4. Place the chicken wings directly on the smoker rack. Smoke for 1½ to 2 hours for crispy wings, checking for an internal temperature of 165°F.

INGREDIENT TIP: Create your own homemade chipotles by smoking jalapeños sprinkled with salt at 250°F for 1½ hours using mesquite wood. Rehydrate as needed.

Perfect tailgate food is handheld! Though you won't catch a buzz from these legs, they definitely have a more grown-up flavor than fried chicken.

DRUNKEN DRUMSTICKS

MAKES 8 TO 12 LEGS | **250°F** | **PECAN**

BRINING TIME: 3 hours
PREP TIME: 45 minutes
SMOKE TIME: 1½ to 2 hours

FOR THE RUB

¼ cup light-brown sugar

2 tablespoons paprika

1¼ teaspoons kosher salt

1 teaspoon cayenne pepper

½ teaspoon garlic powder

½ teaspoon onion powder

¼ teaspoon freshly ground black pepper

FOR THE BEER BARBECUE SAUCE

2 cups ketchup

1 cup beer

⅓ cup chopped onion

2 tablespoons minced garlic

2 tablespoons Worcestershire sauce

2 tablespoons honey Dijon mustard

1 tablespoon molasses

1 tablespoon firmly packed brown sugar

½ teaspoon salt

½ teaspoon freshly ground black pepper

⅓ teaspoon hot sauce

TO MAKE THE SPICE RUB

In a small bowl, mix together the brown sugar, paprika, salt, cayenne, garlic powder, onion powder, and pepper. Set aside.

TO MAKE THE BEER BARBECUE SAUCE

In a medium saucepan over medium-high heat, stir together the ketchup, beer, onion, garlic, Worcestershire sauce, mustard, molasses, brown sugar, salt, pepper, and hot sauce. Bring to a boil, remove from the heat, and let cool.

FOR THE BRINE

1 quart water

2 (12-ounce) bottles of beer

½ cup salt

½ cup firmly packed
brown sugar

8 to 12 chicken legs

Olive oil, for basting

2 tablespoons chopped fresh
parsley leaves

2 tablespoons chopped
fresh chives

TO MAKE THE BRINE

1. In a container large enough to hold the brine and the chicken legs, combine the water and beer.

2. Add the salt and stir until dissolved.

3. Add the brown sugar and stir until dissolved.

4. Add the chicken legs to the container, making sure they are covered with the brine. Cover and refrigerate for 3 hours.

5. Preheat the smoker to 250°F with the pecan wood for indirect heat. Keep the smoke going the entire time for great flavor.

6. Discard the brine and rinse the chicken. Pat the chicken dry with paper towels.

7. Baste the chicken with olive oil, making sure all sides are well coated.

8. Season the chicken generously with the spice rub and sprinkle with the parsley and chives. Place the chicken legs directly on the smoker rack and smoke for 1½ to 2 hours. After about 45 minutes, use an instant-read thermometer to check the temperature, or you can use a thermometer with a leave-in probe to keep you aware of the temperature throughout the smoking process.

9. When the drumsticks reach 160°F, spoon some beer-barbecue sauce onto them. The chicken is done at 165°F.

PREPARATION TIP: Create handles for these drumsticks by trimming the skin off the ends. Use the same method described for the Plum Chicken Pops (see page 50).

In the same way that there are primary colors, Sriracha should be considered a primary food flavor. Sweet, salty, sour, bitter, umami, and Sriracha. I can't get enough.

SWEET SRIRACHA BARBECUE CHICKEN

SERVES 3 OR 4 | **250°F** | **CHERRY**

PREP TIME: 30 minutes
SMOKE TIME: 1½ to 2 hours

1 cup sriracha

½ cup (1 stick) butter

½ cup molasses

½ cup ketchup

¼ cup firmly packed brown sugar

¼ cup prepared yellow mustard

1 teaspoon salt

1 teaspoon freshly ground black pepper

1 whole chicken, cut up

½ teaspoon chopped fresh parsley leaves

1. Preheat the smoker to 250°F with the cherrywood.

2. In a medium saucepan over low heat, stir together the sriracha, butter, molasses, ketchup, brown sugar, mustard, salt, and pepper until the sugar and salt dissolve. Set aside.

3. Divide the sauce into two portions. Brush the chicken with half the sauce and reserve the remaining sauce to serve with the meat. Make sure you divide the sauce *before* basting the chicken, and discard any remaining sauce used to baste the chicken, to eliminate cross-contamination.

4. Place the chicken on the smoker rack and smoke for 1½ to 2 hours, or until an instant-read thermometer reads 165°F.

5. Sprinkle the chicken with the parsley and serve with the reserved barbecue sauce.

PAIR IT: Match the heat of the sriracha pepper with the cool relief of our chilled Smoked Deviled Eggs (page 141).

Applewood has become one of my favorite smoking woods because it immediately reminds me of smoking a Thanksgiving turkey. This breast-only version is perfect for white-meat fans.

APPLEWOOD-SMOKED TURKEY BREAST

SERVES 4 OR 5 | **250°F** | **APPLE**

MARINATING TIME: Overnight
PREP TIME: 20 minutes
SMOKE TIME: 3½ to 4 hours

4 tablespoons unsalted butter, at room temperature

8 teaspoons Dijon mustard

2 tablespoons chopped fresh thyme leaves

1 teaspoon freshly ground black pepper, divided

½ teaspoon kosher salt

1 (6- to 7-pound) bone-in turkey breast

1. In a small bowl, stir together the butter, mustard, thyme, ¼ teaspoon of pepper, and salt. Rub the turkey breast all over with the butter mixture. Cover and refrigerate overnight.

2. Preheat the smoker to 250°F with the applewood.

3. Sprinkle the turkey breast with the remaining ¾ teaspoon of pepper and place it on the smoker rack. Cover and cook for 3½ to 4 hours (about 30 minutes per pound).

4. When a thermometer registers 165°F, remove the turkey from the smoker and let it stand for at least 10 to 15 minutes before serving.

PREPARATION TIP: Turkey skin can act like a wetsuit when it comes to trying to get flavor into the meat. Work the rub under the skin completely first—a technique I call poultry third-base—and you will get the most from the spices combining with the rendered skin.

Jerk seasoning has many different traits. The two standouts are the sweet-and-hot flavor of the Scotch bonnet pepper and the signature smoke of pimento wood. Pimento wood is not easy to find in most parts of the world, but pimento berries are. You know it as allspice, and you can't make jerk chicken without it.

JAMAICAN JERK CHICKEN

SERVES 4 | **275°F** | **MESQUITE**

PREP TIME: 15 minutes
SMOKE TIME: 1½ hours

4 chicken leg quarters, scored

¼ cup canola oil

¼ cup cane syrup

8 whole cloves

6 habanero peppers, sliced

1 scallion, white and green parts, chopped

2 tablespoons whole allspice (pimento) berries, plus more for smoking (see tip)

2 tablespoons salt

2 teaspoons freshly ground black pepper

2 teaspoons ground cinnamon

1 teaspoon cayenne pepper

1 teaspoon dried thyme

1 teaspoon ground cumin

1. Preheat the smoker to 275°F with the mesquite wood. Throw in a handful of whole allspice (pimento) berries with the mesquite.

2. Brush the chicken with the canola oil.

3. In a blender or food processor, combine the cane syrup, cloves, habaneros, scallion, allspice, salt, pepper, cinnamon, cayenne, thyme, and cumin. Pulse until smooth and sticky. Reserve 2 tablespoons of the mixture. Brush the chicken with the remaining mixture, on and under the skin. Place the chicken on the smoker rack and smoke for about 1½ hours.

4. Remove the chicken from the smoker when the internal temperature reaches 160°F, and let the meat stand for about 10 minutes so it reaches the targeted temperature of 165°F by the time you are ready to eat.

5. Baste the chicken with the reserved jerk seasoning before serving.

SMOKING TIP: This recipe uses mesquite instead of the harder-to-find pimento wood. It is a close match for a strong smoke. You can get even closer by adding the dry pimento berries (whole allspice) to your mesquite in the smoker box.

When it comes to cooking low and slow, chicken breast lacks a few of the succulent benefits of brisket and butts. One excellent way to keep chicken just as juicy through a long smoke is by giving it a good bath in a tasty marinade or brine. This one sneaks in an exotic hint of cinnamon.

CINNAMON-CURED FIRE-SMOKED CHICKEN

SERVES 4 | **250°F** | **APPLE OR CHERRY**

BRINING TIME: 1 hour
PREP TIME: 15 minutes
SMOKE TIME: 1½ hours

1 quart water

¼ cup salt

¼ cup firmly packed brown sugar

4 chicken breasts

1 onion, sliced

1 lemon, sliced

2 cinnamon sticks, halved

1 tablespoon ground cinnamon

1 tablespoon red pepper flakes

1 tablespoon seasoned salt

1. In a large bowl, stir together the water, salt, and brown sugar until dissolved.

2. Add the chicken, onion, lemon, and cinnamon sticks. Cover the bowl with plastic wrap and refrigerate for 1 hour.

3. Preheat the smoker to 250°F with the apple or cherrywood.

4. Remove the chicken from the refrigerator and discard the marinade.

5. Sprinkle the chicken with the cinnamon, red pepper flakes, and seasoned salt. Place it on the smoker rack and smoke for about 1½ hours until the internal temperature reaches 165°F.

PREPARATION TIP: Promote crispy skin after brining by rubbing the seasoning under the skin and blotting the skin as dry as possible with a paper towel before placing it in the smoker.

Nothing proclaims family feast as much as a beautifully browned whole turkey on the table. It's more than a meal—it's a work of art.

SMOKY BRINED TURKEY

SERVES 6 TO 8 | **250°F** | **APPLE**

BRINING TIME: Overnight
PREP TIME: 40 minutes
SMOKE TIME: 4 to 5 hours

FOR THE BRINE

2 gallons cold water

1½ cups salt

1¼ cups firmly packed brown sugar

¼ cup freshly ground black pepper

2 tablespoons ground allspice

FOR THE TURKEY

1 (10-pound) fresh whole turkey, neck, giblets, and gizzard removed and discarded

⅓ cup vegetable oil

1 Granny Smith apple, quartered

1 onion, quartered

1 tablespoon dried thyme

½ cup (1 stick) butter, melted

3 tablespoons dried rosemary, divided

TO MAKE THE BRINE

In a container large enough to hold the brine and the turkey, stir together the water, salt, brown sugar, pepper, and allspice until dissolved.

TO MAKE THE TURKEY

1. Fully immerse the turkey in the brine, cover, and refrigerate overnight.

2. Preheat the smoker to 250°F with the applewood.

3. Remove the bird from the brine, drain it well, and pat the skin and inside cavities dry with paper towels. Fold the wingtips behind the back and tie the legs together with kitchen twine.

4. Rub the turkey inside and out with the oil and stuff both the main cavity and the neck with the apple, onion, and thyme. Place the turkey directly on the smoker rack, breast-side up, and smoke for about 3 hours.

5. In a small bowl, stir together the melted butter and rosemary.

6. After about 3 hours, brush the turkey breast with the rosemary butter. Continue to smoke for 1 to 2 hours more. You want an internal temperature of 165°F, but try not to open the smoker any more than you have to as it adds 15 to 20 minutes of cook time every time you do.

7. Remove the turkey from the smoker and let it rest for 20 minutes before carving.

SMOKING TIP: Cooking for a crowd? Instead of going for a 20 pounder, opt for 2 (10-pound) birds. Double the drumsticks—and the turkeys cook faster.

The sweetness of naturally caramelized onions is one of my favorite flavors with mild and sweet chicken breast. Add smoke from a fruitwood such as cherry and the bird flies to a higher level!

CARAMELIZED HONEY BUFFALO CHICKEN

SERVES 4 TO 6 | **250°F** | **CHERRY OR PECAN**

PREP TIME: 20 minutes

SMOKE TIME: 1½ to 2 hours

1 onion, thinly sliced

2 tablespoons butter

½ cup plus 1 tablespoon olive oil, divided

1 cup honey

4 to 6 boneless skinless chicken breasts

1 (5-ounce) bottle Frank's RedHot sauce

Salt

Freshly ground black pepper

1. In a small saucepan over medium-low heat, combine the onion, butter, and 1 tablespoon of olive oil. Sauté the onion for about 15 minutes until caramelized.

2. Stir in the honey and set the sauce aside.

3. Preheat the smoker to 250°F with the cherry or pecan wood.

4. Coat the chicken with the remaining ½ cup of olive oil and generously cover it with some hot sauce. Season with salt and pepper. Place the chicken directly on the smoker rack. Smoke for 1 hour, baste with additional hot sauce and some caramelized onion, and return the chicken to the smoker rack. Total cook time is 1½ to 2 hours, depending on how often you open the smoker lid. Use an instant-read meat thermometer to check for an internal temperature of 165°F.

5. Remove the chicken from the smoker and let it stand for 10 to 15 minutes. Baste with the remaining caramelized onion again before serving.

PAIR IT: Double down on the sweet-onion theme by serving this with our Smoked Onion Bombs (page 133).

The first time I made these pops I overdid the black pepper. The sweetness is the star here, and there's plenty of sugar to handle your experimentation with fiery spices, too. Have plenty of napkins ready. As I like to say, the stickier the better!

PLUM CHICKEN POPS

SERVES 12 | **250°F** | **CHERRY**

PREP TIME: 35 minutes

SMOKE TIME: 2 hours

12 chicken drumsticks

2 teaspoons salt

2 teaspoons freshly ground black pepper

Plum Sauce (page 172)

1. Preheat the smoker to 250°F with the cherrywood.

2. Stretch the skin away from the drumsticks as much as possible and, using a knife and needle-nose pliers, remove the tendons from each leg. The tendons will look like small white laces and can be stubborn to remove.

3. Sprinkle each drumstick with salt and pepper and head to the smoker. Place the chicken on the smoker rack and smoke for about 1½ hours.

4. Lather the pops in plum sauce and return them to the smoker for 30 minutes more until the internal temperature is just under 165°F. The temperature will come up as you let the pops rest for a few minutes.

5. Coat the meat in additional plum sauce to serve.

PREPARATION TIP: Use a paper towel to grasp the legs in step 2 and make sure your pliers (or any other tool you might use to remove the tendons) are properly sanitized (washed in hot, soapy water and thoroughly rinsed and dried).

When all else fails, wrap it in bacon. It is the duct tape of meats!

MESQUITE MAPLE-BACON CHICKEN

SERVES 4 | **250°F** | **MESQUITE**

PREP TIME: 20 minutes

SMOKE TIME: 1½ to 2 hours

4 boneless, skinless chicken breasts

Salt

Freshly ground black pepper

12 bacon slices, uncooked

1 cup maple syrup

½ cup (1 stick) butter, melted

1 teaspoon liquid smoke

1. Preheat the smoker to 250°F with the mesquite wood.

2. Season the chicken with salt and pepper.

3. Wrap each breast with 3 bacon slices to cover the entire surface, and secure with toothpicks.

4. In a medium bowl, stir together the maple syrup, butter, and liquid smoke to make maple butter. Reserve about one-third of the maple butter.

5. Submerge each breast in the maple butter to coat and place it on a grill pan. Place the pan in the smoker and smoke for 1 to 1½ hours.

6. Brush the chicken with the reserved maple butter. Continue to smoke for about 30 minutes more until the internal temperature reaches 165°F.

PAIR IT: While we are wrapping things in bacon, pair this chicken with our Stuffed Jalapeños (page 132) wrapped with another flavor of bacon. Mmmmmm . . . a study in bacon.

Competition Baby Back Ribs, page 58

FOUR

PORK

56 Pork Italian Sausage Fatty

57 Peppercorn Pork Tenderloin

58 Competition Baby
Back Ribs

59 Slow-Smoked Ancho
Chile-Rubbed Boston Butt

61 Homemade Bacon

62 Pig Candy

63 Smoked Sausage Hash

64 Smoked Jalapeño Cheese-
Stuffed Pork Balls

65 Hickory-Smoked Pork Loin

66 Cuban Mojo-Marinated Pork

67 Simple Smoked Pork
Shoulder

68 Carolina Pulled Pork Bites

69 Smoked Italian Sausage

70 Smoked Pork Pinwheels

71 Holiday Ham

When it comes to slow-smoking barbecue in Southern United States, one beast reigns supreme: The humble pig. It's loaded with fat and succulence, and the white meat (still technically considered red meat) absorbs smoke perfectly.

It's a fact that our first Southern US settlers were the inventors of pork barbecue. Christopher Columbus noted in his writing that certain Spanish settlers cooked in a style featuring a grid of green sticks over indirect campfire heat they deemed *barbacoa*. According to some at the South Carolina group DiscoverSouthCarolina.com, it was near Santa Elena (modern-day Parris Island) that the Spanish and American Indians forged barbecue history around a flickering campfire. My pit-master friend and Whole Hog historian Jack Waiboer spelled it out for me. "The Spanish had pigs, and the Indians had developed unique cooking techniques." In those pits is where the magic occurred—swine turned to succulence.

CUTS

Pork remains the slow-smoking leader in the South outside of Texas. To most Southerners, "barbecue" is pulled or chopped smoked pork butt. You should also know that the "butt" is really the shoulder of the pig. And the rear or hindquarter is the ham. Now, if I could fit the whole hog in an electric smoker, I would, as that is the ultimate way to smoke pork. Unfortunately, most smokers are not nearly that big. But a good electric smoker will tackle just about any individual cut from shoulder to belly, butts to bacon, and ribs, too. When you run out of the big cuts, just make sausage. Some of my favorite selections from rib tips to sausage are actually the scraps!

TECHNIQUES

Depending on your favorite cut, there are myriad ways to prepare and season pork. Brines, injections, rubs, and glazes are just the start.

Pork roasts are often injected with a seasoned brine to boost savory flavor. Wrapping butts in aluminum foil near the end of the cook time is also popular. The most popular technique, however, for preparing smoked pork for a crowd is serving it as "pulled pork." This is a Boston butt, whole shoulder, or even an uncured ham that has been fully smoked, then shredded or "pulled" apart into mounds of delicious strands of moist meat and—hopefully—bits of crispy bark. Pork served as pulled reveals meat fibers that are truly tender and moist. Therefore, true pit masters will usually separate and pull by hand. However, if the final product turns out tough they may resort to chopping or mincing. That rat-a-tat-tat of a meat cleaver is a telltale sign of faux tenderness. A bun or white bread is optional.

My favorite rib technique is the 3-2-1 method (see page 58). You smoke your slab for 3 hours, wrap it in foil and cook for 2 more hours, and unwrap and heat for a final hour to firm up the bark. Good things come to those who wait.

Contrary to USDA common advice, most pork is not "done" when it hits an internal temperature of 145°F to 155°F. Sure, it's safe to eat, but a pit master knows that "done" is when the fats, collagen, and connective tissue break down to pull-apart or fall-off-the-bone glory. That magic only happens over 190°F.

You may hear that ribs are sometimes served St. Louis–style. This is a term for trimming a full rack of spare ribs into a tidy elongated rectangle shape. It makes for a nice presentation, but there's nothing wrong with that meat you trim off in the process. I cook it up as a snack.

FINAL TIPS FOR PORK BARBECUE SUCCESS

Great barbecued pork results from high-quality meat, the right temperature, and a long slow cook.

- Better ribs start at the market. Look for meaty slabs and avoid racks with spots of exposed bones or "shiners."

- Pulled pork and ribs need to hit internal temperatures that are much higher than USDA recommendations. Target 205°F for butts to achieve pull-apart tenderness.

- Invest in a quality instant-read electric meat thermometer.

- Enlist the help of a simple sheet of paper towel to grip the membrane and peel it off those ribs.

- Pork ribs come with their own natural "pop-up" thermometer. Look for the ends of the bones to extrude from the meat as a telltale sign of doneness.

- Don't fret about the charred look of your roast. If your electric smoker is working right, it's not burnt. It's bark. And it's amazing.

A fatty is a fairly recent creation in the barbecue world. It's basically a smoked meat loaf, and you can use it as a blank canvas for your favorite flavors. Here, Italian sausage, salami, and marinara combine to create a hearty bite—hold the pasta. Start with very cold meats, as both the sausage and bacon will be extremely difficult to handle at room temperature.

PORK ITALIAN SAUSAGE FATTY

SERVES 4 | **225°F** | **OAK**

PREP TIME: 30 minutes

SMOKE TIME: 2 hours

12 bacon slices

1 pound Italian pork sausage, well chilled

¼ cup marinara sauce, divided

1 cup pepperoni slices

4 slices capicola, well chilled

4 slices genoa salami, well chilled

4 slices ham, well chilled

1 bell pepper (any color), sliced

1 small onion, sliced

½ cup marinated banana peppers, or spicy giardiniera peppers

¼ cup Italian dressing

1. Preheat the smoker to 225°F with the oak wood.

2. On a sheet of plastic wrap, place 6 bacon slices side by side vertically and weave another 6 pieces through them horizontally in an over-under pattern.

3. On another sheet of plastic wrap, spread the sausage to create a circle 10 to 12 inches in diameter.

4. Spread 2 tablespoons of marinara over the sausage round like a pizza, leaving a 1-inch border all the way around.

5. Layer on the pepperoni, capicola, salami, ham, bell pepper, onion, and banana peppers like a pizza, again leaving that 1-inch border.

6. Top with the remaining 2 tablespoons of marinara and sprinkle the Italian dressing over the top.

7. Carefully lift the edges of the sausage round and bring them together. Pinch and press the sausage together to seal the seam and create a stuffed tube. Using the plastic wrap as a support, roll the raw sausage fatty onto the center of the bacon weave. Discard the layer of plastic wrap that was under the sausage.

8. Use the plastic wrap under the bacon to roll and seal the bacon edges around all sides of the sausage roll. Secure with toothpicks and use the plastic wrap to transport it to the smoker grate. Gently roll the fatty so its seam is on the bottom. Smoke for up to 2 hours or until the internal temperature hits 160°F.

PREPARATION TIP: Head to your local sub shop and order up a foot-long Italian sub with double meat—deconstructed—to go. You'll have everything you need to stuff inside this fatty, plus a bonus loaf of bread.

You may not consider it health food, but the pork tenderloin is one of the hog's leanest cuts. It can also potentially get dry, so fill your water pan.

PEPPERCORN PORK TENDERLOIN

SERVES 6 TO 8 | **225°F** | **APPLE**

PREP TIME: 10 minutes

SMOKE TIME: 2 to 3 hours

2 small (1- to 3-pound) pork tenderloins, any remaining silverskin removed

2 tablespoons olive oil

1 tablespoon peppercorns, crushed in a mortar and pestle

2 teaspoons turbinado sugar

1 teaspoon red pepper flakes

1. Preheat the smoker to 225°F with the applewood.

2. Coat the tenderloins with the olive oil.

3. In a small bowl, thoroughly combine the peppercorns, sugar, and red pepper flakes. Rub the spices across the entire surface of each piece of meat. Place both tenderloins in the smoker, allowing for good air and smoke flow. Smoke for 2 to 3 hours, or until the internal temperature reaches 145°F.

4. Let them rest for 10 minutes before slicing and serving.

PAIR IT: For a lighter meal, Smoked Asparagus (page 137) makes a perfect side.

Here's a foolproof trick for barbecue ribs that your guests will rave about. The 3-2-1 method is a simple barbecue trick that works, and it's easy to remember.

COMPETITION BABY BACK RIBS

SERVES 4 | **225°F** | **HICKORY**

PREP TIME: 15 minutes

SMOKE TIME: 3 hours plus 2 hours plus 1 hour

2 full slabs baby back ribs, back membranes removed (use paper towels for a good grip)

1 cup prepared yellow mustard

1 cup Bill's Best Barbecue Rub (page 170)

1 cup apple juice, divided

1 cup brown sugar, divided

1 cup Spicy Hickory-Smoked Barbecue Sauce (page 163), divided

1. Preheat the smoker to 225°F with the hickory wood.

2. Coat the ribs with the mustard to help your favorite rub stick to all parts of the slabs.

3. Coat the ribs with the rub. Place them in the smoker and start with **3 hours** of indirect smoking. This is when you get all the smoke flavor, so use wood (I like hickory) smoke via plenty of hardwood chips.

4. After 3 hours, the smoke should have done most of the "flavoring" that can be absorbed. Now's the time for the "Texas Crutch." It has nothing to do with Texas barbecue, really. Simply put, you wrap and seal each slab individually in heavy-duty aluminum foil. Before sealing the foil wrapping, add ½ cup of apple juice and ½ cup of brown sugar to each pouch. Ride out the next **2 hours** on electric heat—no more woodchips are needed.

5. Finally, unwrap the ribs and coat each slab with ½ cup of the barbecue sauce. Continue to smoke for **1 hour** more while the dry heat tightens the surface of the ribs. Look for a firm, reddish crust or bark and, notably, the meat will clearly pull away from the ends of the bones. Mother Nature's pop-up thermometer!

COOKING TIP: It's difficult to check the internal temperature of pork ribs to see if they are ready to serve. Instead, use a simple toothpick to probe ½ inch into the meat between the ends of two bones. If the pick slides in with very little resistance, they're ready to eat (after a quick rest).

Pork butts, or Boston butt pork roasts, are the tastiest and most efficient cut to use when you're looking for simple pulled pork. The butt is actually from the upper shoulder of the hog. The "butt" in the name comes from the fact that before the Revolutionary War, New England butchers would transport their pork shoulders in barrels called "butts," presumably common for ships in ports such as Boston Harbor. Injecting liquid into the butt, as we do here, enhances the flavor of the meat and keeps it moist. If injecting several butts, double or triple the injection recipe as needed. You want to have plenty.

SLOW-SMOKED ANCHO CHILE-RUBBED BOSTON BUTT

SERVES 10 TO 12 | **200°F, THEN 275°F** | **HICKORY**

MARINATING TIME: Overnight
PREP TIME: 35 minutes
SMOKE TIME: 12½ hours

1 (8- to 10-pound) bone-in pork butt

½ cup prepared yellow mustard

½ cup Bill's Best Barbecue Rub (page 170)

⅓ cup ancho chile powder (if you have time, grind dried peppers to make your own)

½ quart apple juice

½ quart apple cider vinegar

¼ cup salt

1. Generously cover the butt with the mustard and coat well with the rub. Cover and refrigerate overnight. If you are making several butts for a large event, use clean plastic kitchen trash bags and place 2 prepped butts in each.

2. Remove the pork from the refrigerator and let it stand for about 30 minutes to 1 hour to take the chill off the meat. Do not rinse.

3. Preheat the smoker to 200°F with the hickory wood.

4. Coat the outside of the meat with the ancho chile powder.

5. In a large bowl, combine the apple juice, vinegar, and salt. Using a meat injection syringe, inject the pork all over (except on the bottom—it just runs out) with as much liquid as it will hold.

6. Place the butt in the smoker and smoke for about 11 hours.

7. Increase the smoker's temperature to 275°F.

8. Double-wrap the butt tightly with aluminum foil and cook for 1½ hours more. The target internal temperature is about 205°F. Look for a dark, firm bark but with a looseness to the meat indicated by the jiggly looseness of the blade bone. It should pull apart easily.

9. Let the meat rest for 1 hour, then use two forks to pull/shred the pork meat, removing the bone and gristle.

INGREDIENT TIP: A whole shoulder is too large to fit in most electric smokers. If you want some skin still attached to your pork, ask your butcher for the shank end, usually called the picnic shoulder.

You think you love bacon? Nothing quite compares with the passion for cured pork that the organizers of Camp Bacon put on display every year. The annual food festival organizes bacon-themed baking classes featuring bacon doughnuts and cookies, a bacon street fair, plus a food film festival with bacon-enhanced popcorn. If you can't make it to Ann Arbor, Michigan, this year, here's the next best thing: Make bacon at home. Note that the ingredients call for pink curing salt. It is important to use this (also known as Prague powder) to keep the meat from spoiling. Find it and other curing salts in the Resources (page 176). Hickory or applewood gives a nice smokiness to the bacon flavor.

HOMEMADE BACON

MAKES ABOUT 60 SLICES | **200°F** | **APPLE OR HICKORY**

CURING TIME: 8 to 10 days
PREP TIME: 20 minutes
SMOKE TIME: 4 hours

2 tablespoons pink curing salt

2 tablespoons sugar

1 tablespoon freshly ground black pepper

1 (6- to 8-pound) pork belly, skin removed, cut into 3 or 4 pieces

1. In a small bowl, stir together the curing salt, sugar, and pepper.

2. Rub the pork pieces with the spice mixture, and place each piece in a resealable plastic bag or on a dish. Cover tightly. Refrigerate for 8 to 10 days to cure.

3. When ready to smoke, preheat the smoker to 200°F with the apple or hickory wood.

4. Rinse the pork-belly pieces and pat them dry. Place them on the smoker's grill rack and cook for about 4 hours until the internal temperature reaches 150°F.

5. Cool the meat for 30 to 40 minutes. Refrigerate it for several hours before slicing it to your desired thickness.

INGREDIENT TIP: Full pork bellies can weigh in around 12 pounds. A better option for the typical electric smoker is ordering by the pound from a butcher or from most Whole Foods stores. Since you're going all out, look for a specialty pork purveyor and try a premium belly such as Berkshire, Kurobuta, or other heritage breeds.

Warning: You can't un-taste this. Once you experience the sweet, succulent flavor of sticky-and-crispy candied bacon slices you'll never look at bacon the same way again.

PIG CANDY

MAKES 30 TO 40 SLICES | **225°F** | **APPLE, HICKORY, OR MAPLE**

PREP TIME: 20 minutes
SMOKE TIME: 2 hours

Nonstick cooking spray

2 pounds bacon slices (see Homemade Bacon, page 61, if you want to make your own)

1 cup firmly packed brown sugar

2 to 3 teaspoons cayenne pepper

½ cup maple syrup, divided

1. Remove the grill rack from the smoker and cover it with aluminum foil. Use two racks if necessary. Spray the foil with nonstick cooking spray.

2. Lay the bacon out in a single layer, leaving a tiny space between each slice so they don't stick together.

3. In a small bowl, mix together the brown sugar and cayenne, using more or less cayenne to control the heat.

4. Using a brush, generously baste the bacon with ¼ cup of maple syrup.

5. Sprinkle half the rub on top of the bacon.

6. Place the rack(s) in the smoker and smoke the bacon for 1 hour.

7. Flip the bacon, baste this side with the remaining ¼ cup of maple syrup, and sprinkle with the remaining rub.

8. Smoke for 1 hour more until done. The bacon will be brown, firm, and bubbly. Cool and serve, or refrigerate for later use.

PREPARATION TIP: The mind-blowing deliciousness of pig candy is definitely worth the sticky mess left in the smoker. Make cleanup a little easier by using dishwasher-safe Frogmats. They are porous enough to allow smoke to circulate around the meat but catch most of the sticky syrup drippings.

Hash is a general term for a hearty dish of finely chopped meats with spices and onion. The name "hash" actually comes from the French word *hacher*, meaning "to chop."

SMOKED SAUSAGE HASH

SERVES 4 | **225°F** | **APPLE**

PREP TIME: 30 minutes

SMOKE TIME: 45 minutes

Nonstick cooking spray

2 garlic cloves, finely minced

1 teaspoon dried basil

1 teaspoon dried oregano

1 teaspoon onion powder

1 teaspoon salt

1 teaspoon freshly ground black pepper

4 to 6 cooked Smoked Italian Sausage (page 69), sliced

1 large bell pepper (any color), diced

1 large onion, diced

3 potatoes, cut into 1-inch cubes

3 tablespoons olive oil

French bread, for serving

1. Preheat the smoker to 225°F with the applewood.

2. Cover the smoker's grill rack with aluminum foil and coat it with nonstick cooking spray.

3. In a small bowl, mix together the garlic, basil, oregano, onion powder, salt, and pepper.

4. In a large bowl, toss together the sausage slices, bell pepper, onion, potatoes, olive oil, and spice mix to coat. Spread the mixture on the foil-covered rack. Place the rack in the smoker and smoke for about 45 minutes until the potatoes are soft and easily cut with a fork.

5. Serve hot with torn bread.

INGREDIENT TIP: For convenience, use 1 (14-ounce) package of precooked smoked sausage instead of the fresh sausage.

Savory sausage balls are always a hit for tailgate and party appetizers. They are filling and travel well when you're heading away from the patio. These portable bites pack a punch from the jalapeño, so be sure to also have plenty of cold beer on hand.

SMOKED JALAPEÑO CHEESE-STUFFED PORK BALLS

MAKES 2 DOZEN BALLS | **275°F** | **APPLE**

PREP TIME: 30 minutes

SMOKE TIME: 1½ hours

1 (6-ounce) box plain or herb-seasoned Stove Top Stuffing Mix

½ cup hot water

1 pound ground sausage (hot, if desired)

1 egg, lightly beaten

½ cup finely chopped celery

½ cup finely chopped onion

1 jalapeño pepper, seeded and finely chopped (omit if you don't want the heat)

1 cup finely shredded extra-sharp Cheddar cheese

1 pound bacon slices, halved widthwise

Hot Pepper Vinegar Barbecue Sauce (page 165), or Spicy Hickory-Smoked Barbecue Sauce (page 163), for basting and dipping

1. Preheat the smoker to 275°F with the applewood.

2. In a large bowl, combine the stuffing mix and water. Mix well.

3. Add the sausage, egg, celery, onion, jalapeño, and cheese, and blend until all the ingredients are well incorporated. Roll the mixture into 2-inch balls.

4. Wrap each ball with a half slice of bacon, securing with toothpicks. Place the balls on a grill pan and place the pan in the smoker. Smoke for about 1½ hours until the internal temperature hits 165°F.

5. During the last 10 minutes of cook time, glaze the bacon-wrapped balls with the sauce. The glaze will set during the last 10 minutes of cooking.

6. Remove from the heat, lightly baste again, and serve with additional sauce for dipping.

INGREDIENT TIP: Grate or shred your cheese at home. Most prepackaged shredded cheese from the grocery store contains cellulose to keep the cheese from clumping in the bag. Unfortunately, this can also prevent the sausage balls from sticking together.

There are 0 carbs in pork loin, 64 percent protein, and only 154 calories in 4 ounces. This makes "the other white meat" an excellent choice for people watching their waistlines. I really should start doing that.

HICKORY-SMOKED PORK LOIN

SERVES 3 OR 4 | **250°F** | **HICKORY**

BRINING TIME: Overnight
PREP TIME: 15 minutes
SMOKE TIME: 3 hours

½ quart apple juice

½ quart apple cider vinegar

½ cup sugar

¼ cup salt

2 tablespoons freshly ground black pepper

2 teaspoons hickory liquid smoke

1 (4-pound) pork loin roast

½ cup Greek seasoning (Cavender's Greek seasoning is good)

1. In a container large enough to hold the brine and pork, make the brine by combining the apple juice, vinegar, sugar, salt, pepper, and liquid smoke. Stir to dissolve the salt and sugar.

2. Add the loin and enough water to submerge it. Cover and refrigerate overnight.

3. Remove the loin and discard the brine. Do not rinse the meat.

4. Preheat the smoker to 250°F with the hickory wood.

5. Generously coat the meat with the Greek seasoning and place it in the smoker. Smoke for about 3 hours until the internal temperature reaches 160°F.

PREPARATION TIP: Java Rub (page 171) or Bill's Best Barbecue Rub (page 170) work well with this, too.

Of course, Cuba is famous for cigars, but Little Havana also knows food. Cubans take Caribbean ingredients and add Spanish and African flair, pairing some delicious flavors such as avocado, orange, red onion, and lime juice.

CUBAN MOJO-MARINATED PORK

SERVES 8 TO 10 | **225°F** | **APPLE**

MARINATING TIME: Overnight

PREP TIME: 20 minutes

SMOKE TIME: 12 to 14 hours

FOR THE MOJO SAUCE

1 cup freshly squeezed orange juice

½ cup freshly squeezed lime juice

¼ cup olive oil

¼ cup finely minced garlic

1 tablespoon salt

1 tablespoon Mexican adobo seasoning

FOR THE CUBAN RUB

¼ cup Cuban seasoning (I use McCormick)

1 tablespoon onion powder

1 tablespoon garlic powder

Zest of 1 orange, divided

FOR THE PORK

1 (6- to 8-pound) bone-in Boston butt

¼ cup honey

1 avocado, sliced, for serving

1 red onion, thinly sliced, for serving

TO MAKE THE MOJO SAUCE

In a small bowl, stir together the orange juice, lime juice, olive oil, garlic, salt, and adobo seasoning. Set aside.

TO MAKE THE CUBAN RUB

In a small bowl, mix the Cuban seasoning, onion powder, garlic powder, and half of the orange zest. Set aside.

TO MAKE THE PORK

1. Rub the butt with the Cuban rub.

2. With a meat injection syringe, inject the mojo sauce throughout the meat, except on the bottom. Place the meat on a pan and wrap tightly with plastic wrap. Refrigerate overnight.

3. Preheat the smoker to 225°F with the applewood.

4. Remove the meat from the refrigerator and let it come to room temperature. Remove and discard the plastic wrap. Place the meat in the smoker and smoke for 12 to 14 hours until the internal temperature reaches 200°F. Remove from the heat.

5. Drizzle the butt with the honey and the remaining orange zest. Wrap the butt tightly in aluminum foil and place in a cooler to keep warm and rest for about 40 minutes.

6. Cut into chunks and serve with the avocado and red onion slices.

PAIR IT: For a smoking menu, serve this with Hasselback Sweet Potatoes (page 140) and Smoked Mac and Cheese (page 149).

This is the traditional pulled-pork sandwich you've been looking for. A full pork shoulder is a thing to behold, but it can be too large for most electric smokers. The Boston butt and the smaller shank end, a.k.a. the "picnic shoulder," are better choices. Complete your meal with Garlic-Rosemary Potato Wedges (page 136).

SIMPLE SMOKED PORK SHOULDER

MAKES ABOUT 16 SANDWICHES | **200°F** | **HICKORY**

BRINING TIME: Overnight
PREP TIME: 15 minutes
SMOKE TIME: 8 to 9 hours

½ quart apple juice

½ quart apple cider vinegar

½ cup sugar

¼ cup salt

¼ cup soy sauce

1 (5- to 7-pound) picnic pork shoulder roast

¼ cup firmly packed light-brown sugar

1 tablespoon paprika

1 tablespoon ground turmeric

1 tablespoon ground cumin

1½ teaspoons freshly ground black pepper

1 teaspoon dried rosemary

1 teaspoon dried sage

Hot Pepper Vinegar Barbecue Sauce (page 165), for serving

16 hamburger buns

1. In a container large enough to hold the brine and pork, make the brine by combining the apple juice, vinegar, sugar, salt, and soy sauce. Stir to dissolve the sugar and salt.

2. Add the shoulder and enough water to cover the meat. Cover and refrigerate overnight.

3. Remove the shoulder and discard the brine.

4. Preheat the smoker to 200°F with the hickory wood.

5. In a small bowl, mix together the brown sugar, paprika, turmeric, cumin, pepper, rosemary, and sage. Coat the shoulder with this rub and place it in the smoker. Smoke for 8 to 9 hours until the internal temperature reaches 195°F to 205°F, for fall-off-the-bone goodness.

6. Remove the pork and let it rest for 20 minutes. Shred the meat with forks before serving with the buns and sauce.

SERVING TIP: You'll never get a group of barbecue fans to agree on just one favorite sauce. Serve this with a variety of sauces—if you want to be fancy, call it a "study" in sauces.

South and North Carolina disagree when it comes to barbecue sauce. North Carolina leans toward a vinegar base while here in South Carolina we tinker with a mustard-based sweet sauce. It's different than honey mustard but works great on the side as a dip for these pulled-pork bites.

CAROLINA PULLED PORK BITES

MAKES 15 BITES | **250°F** | **PECAN**

PREP TIME: 15 minutes

SMOKE TIME: 2½ hours

1 pound Simple Smoked Pork Shoulder (page 67), pulled

2 cups panko bread crumbs

⅔ cup Carolina Mustard Sauce (page 164), plus more for dipping

1 egg, beaten

1 (8-ounce) block smoked Gouda cheese, cut into 15 cubes

1 pound bacon slices

1. Preheat the smoker to 250°F with the pecan wood.

2. In a large bowl, mix the pork, bread crumbs, sauce, and egg until combined. Roll the mixture to form about 15 meatballs.

3. Push a cheese cube into each meatball and reform into a ball.

4. Wrap a bacon slice around each ball, completely covering it, and place it on a grill pan or Frogmat. Smoke for about 2½ hours until the internal temperature reaches 160°F.

5. Remove from the heat and serve with additional Carolina Mustard Sauce for dipping.

SMOKING TIP: Whenever you smoke meatballs or clusters of smaller appetizers, make sure to allow space between each piece for even smoke flow. Avoid using large sheets of foil under small pieces as it can disrupt air and smoke flow inside the smoker.

For your next cookout, offer Italian sausage for a smoky,
kicked-up "hot dog." Make sure you have enough on hand.
My son, Jack, says one is just a snack; it takes two to be a meal.

SMOKED ITALIAN SAUSAGE

SERVES 6 TO 8 | **250°F** | **APPLE OR HICKORY**

PREP TIME: 5 minutes

SMOKE TIME: 3 to 4 hours

2 pounds (8 to 12 links) Italian
sausage, in casings

8 to 12 hot dog buns

Condiments of choice

1. Preheat the smoker to 250°F with the hickory wood.

2. Place the fresh sausages in their casings on a grill rack. Smoke for
3 to 4 hours until the internal temperature reaches 165°F.

3. Wrap the buns tightly in aluminum foil and stick them in the smoker
for the final 10 to 15 minutes of cook time.

4. Serve the sausages with the heated buns and desired condiments.

SMOKING TIP: Unlike a simple hot dog, fresh sausages hit the smoker
as raw meat. Use care to cook them to the USDA's recommended
temperature of 165°F. I like to keep a warming pan on one side of the
grill and work ahead so as not to get rushed and serve a raw dog.

After rolling up the pinwheels, try dipping them in melted butter and rolling around in crushed pecans for a variation.

SMOKED PORK PINWHEELS

SERVES 15 | **275°F** | **HICKORY**

PREP TIME: 20 minutes

SMOKE TIME: 45 minutes

8 ounces cream cheese, at room temperature

2 tablespoons chopped fresh chives

1 tablespoon garlic powder

2 pounds pork tenderloin, butterflied to lay flat, pounded to ¾ inch thick, and cut into (about 15) long, 1-inch-wide strips

2 teaspoons salt

2 teaspoons freshly ground black pepper

1. Preheat the smoker to 275°F with the hickory wood.

2. In a small bowl, stir together the cream cheese, chives, and garlic powder.

3. Spread each pork strip with a thin amount of the cream-cheese mixture. Roll the strips into pinwheels and secure with toothpicks or kitchen twine.

4. Sprinkle the pinwheels with the salt and pepper and transfer them to a grill pan with a closed bottom. Smoke for about 45 minutes until the internal temperature hits 160°F.

VARIATION TIP: Use this pinwheel idea with flank steak, too. Change the herbs and seasonings in the cream cheese to your taste. The possibilities are endless.

The holiday ham is a work of art worthy of a family gathering. Pineapple rounds and cherries make an elaborate table presentation. But because your ham is cured and precooked, the preparation is a lot easier than it appears ... especially in an electric smoker.

HOLIDAY HAM

SERVES 10 TO 12 | **275°F** | **CHERRY OR HICKORY**

PREP TIME: 35 minutes

SMOKE TIME: 5 hours

2 tablespoons prepared yellow mustard

2 teaspoons hot sauce

1 (5- to 7-pound) precooked bone-in half ham, scored with a sharp knife in straight and parallel lines, making a square pattern

½ cup Bill's Best Barbecue Rub (page 170), divided

1 (14.5-ounce) can sliced pineapple

1 small jar maraschino cherries

Pineapple–Brown Sugar Sauce (page 168)

1. Preheat the smoker to 275°F with the cherry or hickory wood.

2. In a small bowl, stir together the mustard and hot sauce, and spread this on the ham.

3. Generously coat the ham with about 6 tablespoons of the rub.

4. Decorate the ham with pineapple slices and place maraschino cherries in the middle of each slice, secured with toothpicks.

5. Sprinkle the remaining 2 tablespoons of the rub on top of the fruit.

6. Put the ham in the smoker and cook it for about 2 hours.

7. Cover the ham loosely in aluminum foil and continue to smoke for 3 hours more, until the internal temperature reaches 160°F.

8. During the final half-hour of cook time, generously slather the ham with the sauce every 10 minutes, and again just before taking it off the heat.

9. Let the ham rest for 15 to 20 minutes before carving.

10. Serve alongside Smoked Onion Bombs (page 133), if desired.

INGREDIENT TIP: The ham comes from the rear of the hog, unlike the Boston butt, which comes from the top of the shoulder. However, the meaty whole ham has both a butt end and a shank end. The shank end is the lower, more tapered, part of the hindquarter and can be a bit tougher, with a higher percentage of bone and skin. I prefer using the butt half for this feast.

Smoked Tri-Tip Roast, page 76

76 Smoked Tri-Tip Roast

77 Fireball Whiskey Meatballs

79 Unbelievably Moist Brisket

80 Juicy Beef Short Ribs

81 T-Bone Kebabs

82 Smoked Meat Loaf

83 Smoked Prime Rib

84 Smoked Beef Jerky

85 Bourbon-Marinated
Beef Roast

86 Smoked Chuck Roast

87 Smoked Beef Brisket Chili

88 Spicy Korean Rib
Eye Barbecue

89 Smoked Brisket
Grilled Cheese

90 Big McFatty

91 Smoked Brisket and
Cheese Pizza

FIVE

BEEF

When you want the best in beef you have to take a look at what they have cookin' in the Lone Star state. Deep in the heart of Texas, barbecue pride courses through the veins of the pit masters as if their blood were a mop sauce. Texas barbecue is uniquely beef. Brisket is King. Fresh sausage (such as the zesty jalapeño sausages from Kreuz Market) is also world-class. Down there, brisket and clod are always on the menu, but drive across the country and you'll find a lot more smoked beef. Santa Maria tri-tip, meat loaves, jerky, and prime rib are all taken to a new level with the right amount of hardwood smoke effervescence.

I talked beef with country music-star Kix Brooks who did a TV series on great steak joints called *Steak Out*. He pointed out that many of the best chefs season their world-class steaks simply with salt and pepper. "None of these great steak chefs marinated anything. It was all about starting with great beef." He points out, "You can't get that level of quality beef in the grocery store."

CUTS

We've come a long way from old-time butcher shops to today's mail-order options. Now we have beef that's available via the Internet ranging from organic to grass-fed, Wagyu to hormone- and antibiotic-free. The benefits of grass-fed beef include higher omega-3 levels. Wagyu is a Japanese cattle breed renowned for having more tender, more marbled, and more flavorful beef. If you are really out to impress, or need the edge in a barbecue competition, one trick is to buy the best Wagyu brisket from an online purveyor, such as Snake River Farms. You'll pay a premium, but it's a very real secret ingredient.

GOOD GRADES

The USDA has various grading categories for the beef we buy and sell. This is essentially a coding system for fat content as much as it is for three noted parameters: tenderness, juiciness, and flavor. Again, it pretty much equates to fat content in the cut, not qualities relating to breeds, feed (grass or grain), or organic. Here's the breakdown of the grades you've likely seen and a couple you may not.

- **Prime** beef features the most fat marbling and is rarely found in normal supermarkets. You will find it in hotels, restaurants, butchers, and for special order on the Internet.

- **Choice** beef is good quality but with relatively less marbled fat than prime grade.

- **Select** beef is even leaner. Less fat, therefore less juicy and flavorful.

- **Standard and Commercial** beef still make it to the supermarket and are usually "ungraded" or store branded.

- **Utility, Cutter, and Canner** beef won't be found in your grocery's meat section but are sold to manufacturers for processed meat products such as hot dogs and cheap hamburgers.

TECHNIQUES

The three main techniques pit masters employ with beef share one thing: simplicity.

1. **Start with top-quality beef.** It may be a premium breed or simply a better cut. Better is better.

2. **Season simply.** Many of the best chefs from steak houses and brisket smoking masters season beef with nothing but salt and pepper.

3. **It's a wrap.** Wrapping large cuts of beef—typically whole brisket—is common. The meat is wrapped midway through the cook time to help lock in moisture and soften the final product. Use heavy-duty aluminum foil (a.k.a. the Texas Crutch) or traditional pink butcher's paper.

FINAL TIPS FOR BEEF BARBECUE SUCCESS

Keep the following in mind for smokin'-good results:

- **Shop for quality.** The USDA grades of Prime, Choice, and Select mainly denote juicy fat content. Prime is not easily found in supermarkets. A trip to a real butcher is worth the splurge.

- **Don't trim too much.** Fat is flavor. Just trim excessive fat caps.

- **Don't peek.** Avoid opening your smoker to check progress. This drops the cook chamber's temperature and can extend total cook time dramatically—often by 15 to 20 minutes—every time you open the door or lift the lid.

- **Watch your target temperature.** Brisket's internal temperature needs to hit 190°F. Use a thermometer.

- **If you're going to cut it, give it a rest.** To retain those coveted juices, let the meat rest out of the cooker for at least 10 minutes before serving.

In California, the Santa Maria–style tri-tip is the defining pro-tein in smokers. The pit masters of the Santa Maria Valley in central California focus on the triangular-shaped roast from the lower area of the sirloin. Unlike brisket, this beef is best served medium-rare with a unique dry rub. It is not consid-ered complete unless it's served with pinquito beans. This meat is typically wood-fired over a live fire of red oak using a unique and very cool grill grate that can be raised and low-ered to adjust the heat over the fire.

SMOKED TRI-TIP ROAST

SERVES 3 TO 4 | **225°F** | **RED OAK**

MARINATING TIME: 4 hours
PREP TIME: 10 minutes
SMOKE TIME: 2 to 3 hours

¾ cup soy sauce

½ cup rice wine vinegar

½ cup water

¼ cup sesame oil

3 tablespoons firmly packed dark-brown sugar

2 scallions, white and green parts, minced

1 tablespoon sesame seeds

1 teaspoon garlic powder

1 teaspoon red pepper flakes

1 teaspoon freshly ground black pepper

1 (2-pound) tri-tip roast

1. In a medium bowl, stir together the soy sauce, vinegar, water, sesame oil, brown sugar, scallions, sesame seeds, garlic powder, red pepper flakes, and pepper until well blended.

2. Place the roast in a shallow container and pour the marinade over the beef. Cover and refrigerate for a minimum of 4 hours, turning the meat as necessary to coat.

3. Preheat the smoker to 225°F with the red-oak wood.

4. Remove the meat and discard the marinade. Place the roast in the smoker for 2 to 3 hours. The internal temperature needs to be 135°F to 145°F depending on how well done you prefer your meat.

PAIR IT: While traditionally served with pinquito beans, add some Chimichurri Sauce (page 169) and tortillas.

Cinnamon has been in use for a long time. Back in ancient nations it was considered a gift fit for monarchs and gods. These days, it's distilled into shots. Indeed, a little cinnamon goes a long way, so use the cinnamon-flavored whiskey sparingly.

FIREBALL WHISKEY MEATBALLS

MAKES 24 MEATBALLS | **225°F** | **OAK**

PREP TIME: 40 minutes

SMOKE TIME: 1 to 1½ hours

FOR THE FIREBALL BARBECUE SAUCE

2 cups ketchup

½ cup Fireball Cinnamon Whisky

¼ cup molasses

¼ cup firmly packed brown sugar

2 tablespoons olive oil

2 tablespoons apple cider vinegar

2 tablespoons Dijon mustard

2 tablespoons Worcestershire sauce

1 tablespoon garlic powder

1 tablespoon onion powder

Salt

Freshly ground black pepper

TO MAKE THE FIREBALL BARBECUE SAUCE

In a medium saucepan over medium heat, combine the ketchup, whiskey, molasses, brown sugar, olive oil, vinegar, mustard, Worcestershire sauce, garlic powder, and onion powder. Season with salt and pepper. Bring to a boil and simmer for 20 to 30 minutes. Remove from the heat and set aside.

FIREBALL WHISKEY MEATBALLS *continued*

FOR THE MEATBALLS

1 pound lean ground beef

1 pound ground pork

1 egg, beaten

½ cup finely chopped onion

½ cup panko bread crumbs

¼ cup shredded
mozzarella cheese

¼ cup grated Parmesan cheese

2 tablespoons tomato paste

2 tablespoons Fireball
Cinnamon Whisky

1 tablespoon Italian seasoning

1 tablespoon minced garlic

1 teaspoon salt

1 teaspoon freshly ground
black pepper

2 teaspoons red pepper flakes

12 bacon slices, cooked
and crumbled

½ cup chopped fresh
parsley leaves

TO MAKE THE MEATBALLS

1. Preheat the smoker to 225°F with the oak wood.

2. In a large bowl, combine the ground beef and pork with the egg, onion, bread crumbs, mozzarella, Parmesan, tomato paste, whiskey, Italian seasoning, garlic, salt, pepper, red pepper flakes, and bacon. Using your hands, mix until well incorporated and roll into 24 balls.

3. Place a Frogmat nonstick grill mat directly on the grate. Arrange the meatballs on the mat leaving space between them for good air and smoke flow. Smoke for 1 to 1½ hours. During the last 15 minutes of cooking, brush the meatballs with some of the barbecue sauce.

4. When an instant-read thermometer registers 160°F, remove the meatballs from the smoker.

5. Sprinkle with the parsley and serve hot with the remaining fireball barbecue sauce.

PAIR THIS: This spicy appetizer is delicious with Baba Ghanouj (page 124) and Stuffed Jalapeños (page 132), and it's great for game-day bites.

Brisket is the daddy of all smoked meats. Originally considered a cheap and tough cut of meat, it is now thought a delicacy. The massive cut is from the chest of the cow and features two parts called the point and the flat.

UNBELIEVABLY MOIST BRISKET

SERVES 8 TO 12 | **225°F** | **OAK**

MARINATING TIME: Overnight
PREP TIME: 30 to 40 minutes
SMOKE TIME: 8 to 10 hours

1 cup kosher salt

1 cup coarsely ground black pepper

1 (8- to 12-pound) brisket, trimmed of hardened fat thicker than ½ inch

2 cups prepared yellow mustard

1. Preheat the smoker to 225°F with the oak wood for indirect heat.

2. In a medium bowl, mix together the salt and pepper.

3. Slather the brisket with the mustard to act as an adherent.

4. Coat the entire surface of the meat with the salt-and-pepper blend. It's a lot of salt and pepper but a roast this size uses it nicely.

5. Arrange the meat in the center for your smoker, fat-side up. If the whole brisket won't fit, use a sharp knife to trim off the point by following the flat's fat cap, to make a second roast. Smoke for 4 to 5 hours (typically) until the internal temperature reaches about 165°F.

6. Following Texas tradition, wrap the meat tightly with pink butcher's paper to seal in the juices. Continue to cook to an internal temperature of around 205°F, typically 4 to 5 hours more. Smoke is no longer a big factor. Look for a dark mahogany bark and a spring to the touch.

7. Remove the meat from the smoker, uncover it, and let it rest off the heat for up to 1 hour before slicing.

8. Separate the point and reserve for burnt ends, if desired (see tip). Slice the flat against the grain in pencil-thin slices.

9. Serve with Smoked Cauliflower Steaks (page 145), if desired.

INGREDIENT TIP: Burnt ends are choice morsels created by cutting chunks from the fattier "point" side of the brisket after it has been fully cooked, coating the pieces with sauce, and smoking them for an additional hour. Competition pit masters work to include these flavorful pieces, and judges dream of getting them in a turn-in box!

I cannot think of beef ribs without good ol' Fred Flintstone coming to mind. He was the original pit master! His giant slab was so heavy it tipped over his car. That is how I think about beef ribs. If you cooked the whole rib bone you'd be just like Fred. However, by definition, beef short ribs are a shortened portion of the entire rib bone. You can make them easier to handle by serving them flanken-style, cut across the bone about ½ inch thick and in 2-inch or shorter lengths, or English-style with the bones cut in 6-inch lengths.

JUICY BEEF SHORT RIBS

SERVES 4 OR 5 | **225°F** | **MESQUITE OR OAK**

PREP TIME: 10 to 15 minutes

SMOKE TIME: 3 to 4 hours

8 to 10 English-cut beef short ribs

¼ cup olive oil

½ cup apple cider vinegar

½ cup apple juice

Java Rub (page 171)

1. Preheat the smoker to 225°F with the mesquite or oak wood.

2. Trim some of the fat off the ribs and rub the ribs with the olive oil.

3. In a kitchen spray bottle, mix the vinegar and apple juice together.

4. Coat the ribs with the rub and head outside. Place the ribs in the smoker and smoke for 1 hour. Spray them with the vinegar-and-apple-juice mixture. Smoke for about 2 hours more, spraying the ribs every 15 to 20 minutes until done. Total cook time should be 3 to 4 hours with a target temperature of 175°F to 205°F. The ribs will appear beautifully browned and, if cooked to the higher temperature, will be falling off the bone.

5. Serve with Smoked Bacon-Wrapped Onion Rings (page 138), if desired.

PREPARATION TIP: The membrane on the inside of the rib slab can be difficult to remove, but it must be removed, unlike with pork ribs where membrane removal is optional. Grab a blunt knife to pry up a flap to grasp with a paper towel and pull.

The T-bone is a great grilling steak—with two beautiful cuts in one. You enjoy both the smaller tenderloin and a larger nicely marbled New York strip. Since you are smoking these, look for an "off the bone" strip with just a bit of tenderloin, which you might get for a better price.

T-BONE KEBABS

MAKES 8 SKEWERS | 225°F | OAK

MARINATING TIME: 4 to 8 hours

PREP TIME: 20 minutes

SMOKE TIME: 45 minutes to 1 hour

1 pound beef tenderloin, cut into 1-inch cubes

2 pounds strip steak, cut into 1-inch cubes

1 large onion, cut into 1-inch cubes

1 bell pepper (any color), cut into 1-inch cubes

1 zucchini, cut into 1-inch cubes

1 pint (about 10 ounces) cherry tomatoes

¼ cup olive oil

½ cup steak seasoning

1. In a large bowl, combine the tenderloin, strip steak, onion, bell pepper, zucchini, and tomatoes with the olive oil and steak seasoning. Gently stir until coated. Cover and refrigerate for 4 to 8 hours.

2. When ready to smoke, preheat the smoker to 225°F with the oak wood.

3. Make the kebabs by alternating different veggies and meat on your skewers, beginning and ending with meat. Transfer the skewers to a grill rack and smoke for 45 minutes to 1 hour. Remove from the smoker when the internal temperature of the steak is at least 135°F (rare) or 140°F (medium-rare).

SMOKING TIP: Soak wooden skewers in water before smoking to avoid burning. Double-skewer for easy handling and to prevent the spinning of the ingredients.

Look up "comfort food" in the dictionary and you just might see a photo of the humble meat loaf. Hearty. Filling. Delightfully retro. Add the flavor of hardwood smoke to the recipe and it graduates from comfort food to luxury feast.

SMOKED MEAT LOAF

SERVES 4 TO 6 | **225°F** | **OAK**

PREP TIME: 20 minutes

SMOKE TIME: 2 hours

FOR THE SAUCE

½ cup ketchup

½ cup firmly packed brown sugar

2 teaspoons salt

1 teaspoon freshly ground black pepper

1 teaspoon cayenne pepper

FOR THE MEAT LOAF

Nonstick cooking spray

1 pound ground beef

1 pound ground pork

1 small onion, chopped

2 eggs, beaten

½ cup panko bread crumbs

⅓ cup milk

2 tablespoons Worcestershire sauce

1 tablespoon minced garlic

1½ teaspoons salt

1½ teaspoons freshly ground black pepper

TO MAKE THE SAUCE

In a small bowl, stir together the ketchup, brown sugar, salt, pepper, and cayenne. Set aside.

TO MAKE THE MEAT LOAF

1. Preheat the smoker to 225°F with the oak wood.

2. Grease an 8½-by-4½-inch loaf pan with nonstick cooking spray and set aside.

3. In a large bowl, combine the beef, pork, onion, eggs, bread crumbs, milk, Worcestershire sauce, garlic, salt, and pepper. With clean hands, mix the ingredients until well incorporated. Form the meat mixture into a loaf and place it in the prepared pan.

4. Smoke the meat loaf for about 2 hours, glazing it with the sauce during the final 30 minutes of cook time. Once the meat loaf hits an internal temperature of 165°F, the top should look and feel firm and have a reddish glaze.

SMOKING TIP: Yes, you should let even meat loaf rest after cooking, just like other roasts. Tent under aluminum foil for 10 minutes and you'll be in the "comfort zone."

If you're ready to eat like all-out royalty, try smoking this standing rib roast—a.k.a. prime rib. Despite the common name, the USDA does not require the cut to be of a "prime" grade beef.

SMOKED PRIME RIB

SERVES 8 TO 10 | **225°F** | **OAK**

MARINATING TIME: 4 hours

PREP TIME: 25 minutes

SMOKE TIME: 4 to 6 hours

1 (4-bone, about 8-pound) prime rib roast (see tip)

2 onions, thickly sliced

Smoky Teriyaki Marinade (page 173)

Salt

Freshly ground black pepper

1. In a container large enough to hold the meat and marinade, combine the roast and onion slices. Pour the marinade over. Cover tightly and refrigerate to marinate for 2 hours.

2. Turn the meat over, replace the lid, and refrigerate for 2 hours more.

3. Preheat the smoker to 225°F with the oak wood.

4. Remove the roast and onions from the container and discard the marinade.

5. Skewer the onion slices to make "onion lollipops."

6. Season the prime rib on both sides with salt and pepper. Place the meat and onions on the smoker rack.

7. Smoke the meat for 4 to 6 hours and the onions until done (about 2 hours).

8. Remove the prime rib from the smoker when the internal temperature reaches at least 135°F. Let it rest for 15 minutes. Serve with the onion lollipops.

PREPARATION TIP: Before smoking the meat, trim the thin blue muscle (tapered and larger on one side) off the top and discard.

Making jerky originally developed as a method for preserving meat, but jerky is also popular as a nutrient-packed travel food. Far from health food, it's still nutritious, packing a lot of protein and sustenance in a small, light package. Plus, it's popular with backpackers, in military rations, and as astronaut space food. So you're in very cool company.

SMOKED BEEF JERKY

MAKES ABOUT 25 PIECES | **180°F** | **HICKORY**

MARINATING TIME: 4 to 6 hours

PREP TIME: 30 minutes

SMOKE TIME: 4 to 5 hours

2 pounds flank steak, pounded to an even ½-inch thickness

½ cup soy sauce

½ cup apple cider vinegar

¼ cup Worcestershire sauce

2 tablespoons dry minced onion

1 tablespoon honey

2 teaspoons freshly ground black pepper, plus more for seasoning

1 teaspoon liquid smoke

1 teaspoon red pepper flakes

1. Cut the meat across the grain into about 25 strips.

2. In a large shallow dish, mix the soy sauce, vinegar, Worcestershire sauce, onion, honey, 2 teaspoons of pepper, liquid smoke, and red pepper flakes. Add the meat, stir to coat, cover, and refrigerate to marinate for 4 to 6 hours.

3. Preheat the smoker to 180°F with the hickory wood.

4. Remove the meat from the dish and discard the marinade. Pat the meat dry with paper towels and place it in a single layer on a grill pan.

5. Sprinkle with additional pepper and smoke for 4 to 5 hours until the jerky appears dry and leathery.

6. Blot dry with paper towels and keep refrigerated for up to 1 month (if it lasts that long!).

SMOKING TIP: Your electric smoker will also make tender beef snack sticks. Marinate 2 pounds of lean (90/10) ground beef in the same marinade as in the preceding recipe (or feel free to change up the spices). Use a jerky gun to make the strips, and smoke. You'll get beef sticks that will have Slim Jim running to Mommy.

Bourbon is popular in Kentucky. They celebrate it in Bardstown with a Bourbon Festival and commemorate September as Bourbon Heritage Month. I have no problems with anyone enjoying a glass straight up, but with bourbon's complex flavor profile, you really should try it in a recipe. Southern chefs use more than just a splash in recipes for everything from pies to salad dressings. With its sweetness and earthy character, it goes well with a lot of barbecue and adds the perfect touch to this beef marinade.

BOURBON-MARINATED BEEF ROAST

SERVES 3 OR 4 | **225°F** | **APPLE, HICKORY, OR OAK**

MARINATING TIME: Overnight
PREP TIME: 15 minutes
SMOKE TIME: 1 hour per pound

½ cup firmly packed light-brown sugar

½ cup soy sauce

½ cup olive oil

¼ cup bourbon

Juice of 1 lemon

1 tablespoon freshly ground black pepper

1 (3- to 4-pound) beef roast

1. In a medium bowl, whisk together the brown sugar, soy sauce, olive oil, bourbon, lemon juice, and pepper to make the marinade.

2. In a large bowl, combine the meat and marinade. Cover loosely with plastic wrap and refrigerate overnight.

3. Preheat the smoker to 225°F with the apple, hickory, or oak wood.

4. Remove the meat from the bowl and discard the marinade. Place the roast on the smoker rack and smoke for 1 hour per pound. Remove from the heat when the internal temperature reaches 145°F.

INGREDIENT TIP: You may be tempted to reuse this marinade after the overnight soak. *Don't.* Once in contact with raw meat the liquid can easily harbor harmful bacteria and by-products the bacteria leave behind. Toss it.

The affordable chuck roast is most famously used for slow-cooked fall-apart pot roast. Here we smoke it like Texas beef shoulder clod, as it comes from the same general area of the cow. Chuck roasts are readily available in most supermarkets and can be a more convenient size than a whole shoulder or a whole brisket.

SMOKED CHUCK ROAST

SERVES 4 TO 6 | **225°F** | **MESQUITE AND OAK**

PREP TIME: 15 minutes

SMOKE TIME: 1 hour per pound

1 (4- to 5-pound) chuck roast

¼ cup olive oil

¼ cup firmly packed brown sugar

2 tablespoons Cajun seasoning

2 tablespoons paprika

2 tablespoons cayenne pepper

1. Preheat the smoker to 225°F with the mesquite or oak wood.

2. Rub the chuck roast all over with the olive oil.

3. In a small bowl, mix together the brown sugar, Cajun seasoning, paprika, and cayenne. Coat the roast generously with the spice mix.

4. Place the roast on the smoker rack and smoke for 1 hour per pound. Remove from the heat when the internal temperature reaches 165°F. This temperature works well for meat that will be sliced.

5. If you desire a more traditional fall-apart texture (some even serve this pulled) continue to smoke to an internal temperature of 180°F to 190°F. Wrap with aluminum foil and let it rest for 30 minutes.

PAIR IT: Serve with Chimichurri Sauce (page 169) on the side.

The secret to this chili is the finely diced burnt brisket ends that take regular chili to another level. Now all you need is enough self-control to save a couple pounds of leftover brisket!

SMOKED BEEF BRISKET CHILI

SERVES 6 TO 8

PREP TIME: 20 minutes

COOK TIME: 1 to 2 hours

1 tablespoon olive oil

1 small onion, chopped

2 garlic cloves, minced

½ cup chili powder (Feeling adventurous? See the tip for homemade chili powder.)

1 large fresh poblano pepper, fire-roasted and seeded

1 (28-ounce) can crushed tomatoes

1 (15-ounce) can kidney beans, rinsed and drained

1 (12-ounce) bottle robust beer

2 beef bouillon cubes

1 tablespoon salt

2 teaspoons smoked paprika

2 teaspoons ground cumin

1½ teaspoons cayenne pepper

2 pounds leftover Unbelievably Moist Brisket (page 79), chopped

1. In a soup pot over medium-high heat, heat the olive oil and sauté the onion and garlic for about 3 minutes until translucent.

2. Add the chili powder, poblano, tomatoes, kidney beans, beer, bouillon cubes, salt, paprika, cumin, and cayenne. Stir to combine and bring to a boil. Reduce the heat to low and simmer for 1 to 2 hours.

3. Stir in the brisket and heat through before serving.

INGREDIENT TIP: Make better chili powder: In a dry pan, lightly toast 2 ounces dried guajillo chiles, 1 ounce dried árbol chiles, and 2 ounces dried ancho chiles with 5 tablespoons cumin seeds, until fragrant. Grind the toasted ingredients into a powder using a spice grinder. Add 2 tablespoons granulated garlic, ¼ cup dried oregano, and ¼ cup smoked paprika. The freshness puts the store-bought stuff to shame.

The rib eye is a classic cowboy steak that takes to wood smoke nicely. In fact, in the United States it's called a cowboy rib eye when served with the bone in. In Australia, if you remove the bone it's called a Scotch fillet. We're slicing these to serve nestled in tortillas, so shop for boneless rib eye. I use peach or pear woodchips to smoke to add some sweet, fruity flavor to complement the spicy Korean kick.

SPICY KOREAN RIB EYE BARBECUE

SERVES 4 | **200°F** | **PEACH OR PEAR**

PREP TIME: 10 minutes

SMOKE TIME: 15 minutes per pound

¼ cup soy sauce

¼ cup chopped scallion, white and green parts

2 tablespoons minced garlic

2 tablespoons gochujang Korean chili paste

1 tablespoon honey

2 teaspoons ground ginger

2 teaspoons onion powder

2 (8- to 12-ounce) boneless rib eye steaks

Smoked Coleslaw (page 131)

12 flour tortillas

1. Preheat the smoker to 200°F with the peach or pear wood.

2. In a small bowl, whisk the soy sauce, scallion, garlic, gochujang, honey, ginger, and onion powder to make a paste. Spread the paste on both sides of the steaks.

3. Place the steaks in the smoker and smoke for about 15 minutes per pound. Remove from the heat when the internal temperature reaches 115°F to 120°F, and quickly sear on both sides on a hot grill or in a skillet. Final temperature is a matter of taste, with 145°F suggested by the USDA for medium-rare.

4. Cut the steaks into strips and serve with the coleslaw all wrapped in the flour tortillas.

PAIR IT: Kick up your meal some more with spicy Stuffed Jalapeños (page 132).

There is more to grilled cheese than just a frying pan and processed American cheese. Here's a chance to repurpose a bit of brisket and smoked cheese from your electric smoker's finest moments. You call it leftovers; I call it a smoker's greatest hits.

SMOKED BRISKET GRILLED CHEESE

MAKES 4 SANDWICHES | **275°F** | **CHERRY**

PREP TIME: 15 minutes

SMOKE TIME: 15 to 20 minutes

8 slices thick-sliced French bread

Pineapple–Brown Sugar Sauce (page 168)

4 tablespoons soft, spreadable herbed goat cheese (chèvre)

2 ounces Gruyère cheese, thinly shaved

4 thick slices Unbelievably Moist Brisket (page 79)

4 slices smoked Cheddar cheese

4 or 8 tomato slices

1 avocado, peeled, pitted, and sliced

4 tablespoons (½ stick) butter, melted

Dill pickle slices, for serving

1. Preheat the smoker to 275°F with the cherrywood.

2. Slather one side of each bread slice with the pineapple sauce and place on the smoker's grill rack sauce-side down. Lightly smoke the bread for about 5 minutes, then flip it.

3. Spread the sauced side of four bread slices with the goat cheese and top the remaining four "bottom buns" with the Gruyère. Smoke for 5 to 10 minutes more.

4. When the cheese begins to melt, top the Gruyère-side bread with the brisket. Top the brisket with the Cheddar.

5. Place 1 or 2 tomato slices and avocado slices on top of the Cheddar. Place the remaining bread slices on top, brush with the melted butter, and smoke for about 5 more minutes.

6. Serve with dill pickle slices.

SMOKING TIP: Grilling bread is touchy on a hot and fast grill—it will burn up in a split second. Smoking gives you greater control. Place the bread near the bottom of the smoker's heating element and increase the heat (if possible) in the final minute to encourage browning of the bread and butter.

You probably remember the song with all the Big Mac ingredients. That will make it easy for you to memorize the basics of this fatty that skips the bun, but brings back all the flavors of a fast-food classic. Just add smoke.

BIG MCFATTY

SERVES 6 TO 8 | **250°F** | **HICKORY**

PREP TIME: 25 minutes
SMOKE TIME: 2 hours

FOR BILL'S SPECIAL SAUCE
¼ cup mayonnaise
¼ cup Miracle Whip
3 tablespoons French dressing
1½ tablespoons dill-pickle relish
1½ teaspoons sweet
pickle relish
1 teaspoon sugar
1 teaspoon dry minced onion
1 teaspoon vinegar
1 teaspoon ketchup
Pinch salt

FOR THE FATTY
1 pound bacon slices
2 pounds ground beef
Salt
Freshly ground black pepper
½ cup dill-pickle slices
4 slices American cheese
1 onion, sliced
2 tablespoons sesame
seeds, divided

TO MAKE BILL'S SPECIAL SAUCE
In a small microwave-safe bowl, stir together the mayonnaise, Miracle Whip, French dressing, dill and sweet relishes, sugar, onion, vinegar, ketchup, and salt. Microwave on high power for 30 seconds and stir. Refrigerate until needed.

TO MAKE THE FATTY
1. Preheat the smoker to 250°F with the hickory wood.

2. Line a rimmed baking sheet with parchment paper. On the sheet, place 6 bacon slices side by side vertically and weave another 6 pieces through them horizontally in an over-under pattern.

3. Layer the ground beef on top to cover the bacon.

4. Season with salt and pepper.

5. Layer the pickles, American cheese, and onion on the ground beef, leaving a 1-inch border all the way around. Using the parchment paper as an aid, roll the fatty into a roll (think sushi).

6. Spread half of the sauce on the fatty, sprinkle with 1 tablespoon of sesame seeds, and transfer to the smoker. Smoke for about 2 hours, or until the internal temperature reaches 160°F.

7. Top with the remaining sauce and 1 tablespoon of sesame seeds. Let the fatty rest for a few minutes.

8. Slice to serve (an electric carving knife works well).

PAIR IT: A potato side is perfect, such as Potato Bacon Bites (page 143) or Garlic-Rosemary Potato Wedges (page 136).

For true wood-fired pizza you need higher temperatures than you can achieve with the typical electric smoker. Not to be deterred, we solve that problem by starting with a prepared pizza crust, topping it with a premium melty cheese, and allowing the smoke to add the flavor of an artisanal wood-fired pizza oven. Mesquite or hickory woodchips will give it great flavor.

SMOKED BRISKET AND CHEESE PIZZA

SERVES 2 OR 3 | **275°F** | **HICKORY OR MESQUITE**

PREP TIME: 15 to 20 minutes

SMOKE TIME: 1 to 1½ hours

1 tablespoon butter

1 tablespoon all-purpose flour

½ cup cold milk

2 garlic cloves, minced

¼ teaspoon salt

⅛ teaspoon freshly ground black pepper

⅛ teaspoon ground nutmeg

¼ cup grated Parmesan cheese

1 (12-inch) Boboli pizza crust (or use a smaller size for individual pizzas)

1 cup leftover chopped smoked brisket

½ onion, sliced

½ bell pepper (any color), sliced

½ cup (torn thin strips) provolone cheese

½ cup (torn thin strips) white American cheese

1. Preheat the smoker to 275°F with the hickory or mesquite wood.

2. In a saucepan over medium heat, make a roux by melting the butter, adding the flour, and whisking continuously for about 1 minute.

3. Slowly pour in the cold milk while continuing to whisk.

4. Add the garlic, salt, pepper, and nutmeg, and continue stirring until thickened.

5. Remove from the heat and stir in the Parmesan cheese until it has melted and is fully incorporated. Remove from the heat and let the sauce cool.

6. Spread the cooled sauce over the crust. Layer on the brisket, onion, and bell pepper. Sprinkle the provolone and American cheeses on top.

7. Place the pizza directly on the smoker rack or on a Frogmat grill mat and smoke for 1 to 1½ hours until the veggies are tender and the cheeses are bubbly.

PREPARATION TIP: If you want to skip the process of making a roux, buy a jarred Alfredo sauce at your local supermarket to use as the base and skip steps 2 through 5.

Maple-Glazed Salmon, page 96

95 Lemon Pepper
    Bacon-Wrapped Trout

96 Maple-Glazed Salmon

97 Succulent Salmon
    Nuggets

98 Peppercorn Tuna Steaks

99 Smoked Halibut

100 Country Cajun Catfish

101 Sugared Sea Bass

102 Smoked Lobster Tails

103 Scuppernong Lobster

104 Smoky Oysters

105 Smoked Shrimp and
    Scallops

106 Citrus and Garlic Scallops

107 Cajun Shrimp

108 Bacon-Wrapped
    Crab-Stuffed Shrimp

109 Crab-Stuffed Tomato

SIX

FISH & SEAFOOD

When you think about smoked fish, salmon is the go-to dish. But there's an endless variety of seafood that absorbs smoke incredibly well. The general rule is that the fattier the fish, the more the smoky flavor will be absorbed. Salmon and trout have high fat content and are perfect for the electric smoker because it can easily maintain the lower, sub-200°F temperatures to allow the fish to slowly absorb the subtle flavors without overcooking the delicate meat.

As with smoked meats, the process of smoking fish started as a way of cooking and preserving the food, and the powerful flavors and superior health benefits have continued to stand the test of time.

CUTS

I have always considered seafood a summer-time food. However, these days there are many different kinds of fish available year-round. Smoked shrimp and lobster are luxurious smoking experiments you can easily tackle in any season. With a feast of smoked fish or shellfish you can create your idea of the perfect summer beach meal even in the dead of winter.

So which are the best cuts and kinds of seafood for smoking? My suggestion is to think local. Here in Charleston I suggest some South Carolina shrimp. In the Pacific North you have to go with salmon. Sourcing close to home helps keep things fresh!

FINAL TIPS FOR FISH AND SEAFOOD BARBECUE SUCCESS

Some things to remember:

- Choose thin-skinned fish for the best absorption of smoke flavors.

- Carefully inspect fish such as salmon and trout for pin bones before preparing.

- Use parchment paper, aluminum foil, or Frogmats to minimize sticking of the fish to the thin grates of the smoker.

- Place the fish skin-side down on the grate.

- Delicate meats call for a more delicate wood flavor so you'll use citrus and fruit-woods, alder, and sometimes cedar planks.

- Purchase a fish spatula—a slotted, offset, flexible spatula that is the perfect tool for lifting and moving delicate foods.

- The racks in your electric smoker are easily removable. Transfer full racks to a clean food-prep area for easier handling and to keep from overhandling delicate cuts.

A note on smoked salmon: There are lots of varieties of smoked salmon, including the cured cold-smoked and cooked hot-smoked salmon. But to many people's surprise, lox is *not* smoked—just salt-brined.

Trout are generally plentiful and, as members of the salmon family, they grow fairly large. The biggest rainbow trout on record was caught in 2009 in Canada, weighing in at 48 pounds!

LEMON PEPPER BACON-WRAPPED TROUT

SERVES 4 | **200°F** | **ALDER, APPLE, OR CHERRY**

PREP TIME: 15 minutes

SMOKE TIME: 2 to 2½ hours

4 trout fillets

1 tablespoon freshly ground black pepper

2 teaspoons salt

4 to 8 bacon slices, partially cooked

Juice of 1 lemon

Chopped fresh parsley leaves, for garnish

1. Preheat the smoker to 200°F with alder, apple, or cherrywood.

2. Generously season the fillets with the salt and pepper before wrapping each with 1 or 2 bacon slices, depending on the size of the fish. Wrap the bacon tightly and secure the ends as tightly as possible.

3. Squeeze lemon juice on all sides of the fillets, and head to the smoker.

4. Place the fish in the smoker and smoke for 2 to 2½ hours until the fish reaches an internal temperature of 160°F. The flesh should be soft yet flaky when gently pressed with a fork.

5. Sprinkle with parsley and serve warm.

INGREDIENT TIP: I'm always surprised at the dozens of bacon choices at the supermarket. Avoid purchasing a (common) hickory-smoked bacon that may conflict with your chosen smoking wood.

Found in the Atlantic and Pacific Ocean, most salmon are born in fresh water but migrate to the sea and return to fresh water to reproduce. Interestingly, they change color when going from fresh water to salt water.

MAPLE-GLAZED SALMON

SERVES 10 TO 12 │ **250°F** │ **ALDER OR CEDAR PLANKS**

MARINATING TIME: 8 hours or overnight

PREP TIME: 15 minutes, plus 1 hour

SMOKE TIME: 1 to 2 hours

2 cups firmly packed brown sugar

½ cup salt

¼ cup maple syrup

3 ounces crab boil seasoning

1 (3- to 5-pound) whole salmon fillet

Chopped fresh parsley leaves, for garnish

Cream cheese, for serving

1. In a medium bowl, mix the brown sugar, salt, maple syrup, and crab boil into a paste. Rub the paste all over the salmon and place the salmon in a shallow dish. Cover and refrigerate for a minimum of 8 hours or overnight.

2. Remove the salmon from the refrigerator and let it sit for 1 hour to take the chill off.

3. Preheat the smoker to 250°F with the alder wood. Cedar planks work great, especially if you are smoking smaller fillets.

4. Place the salmon on the smoker rack (or cedar plank) and smoke for 1 to 2 hours. The target temperature is 145°F. It's done when it flakes easily with a fork.

5. Remove from the heat, sprinkle with parsley, and serve with cream cheese.

INGREDIENT TIP: Do not overcook the salmon or you will end up with albumin protein (soft white stuff) on the outside of the fish. It comes from the muscle fibers during the cooking process. It will not harm you but it will mar your presentation.

Atlantic salmon are all farm-raised in the United States. They are also known as black salmon, which is now on the endangered list. If you're looking for wild salmon, buy Pacific. Pink salmon is the easiest to find, and actually the smallest, usually weighing between 3 and 5 pounds.

SUCCULENT SALMON NUGGETS

SERVES 4 TO 6 | **180°F** | **ALDER**

MARINATING TIME: Overnight
PREP TIME: 20 minutes
SMOKE TIME: 1 to 2 hours

3 cups firmly packed brown sugar

1 cup salt

1 tablespoon dry minced onion

2 teaspoons chipotle seasoning

2 teaspoons freshly ground black pepper

1 garlic clove, minced

1 to 2 pounds salmon fillets, cut into bite-size chunks

1. In a large bowl, stir together the brown sugar, salt, onion, chipotle seasoning, pepper, and garlic.

2. Place the salmon in a large, shallow marinating dish and pour the dry marinade over the fish. Cover and refrigerate overnight.

3. Preheat the smoker to 180°F with the alder wood.

4. Rinse the salmon chunks thoroughly to remove the salt. Place them on a grill rack and put them into the smoker. Smoke for 1 to 2 hours. Remove from the heat when the internal temperature is 130°F to 140°F.

PAIR IT: For a party with heavy hors d'oeuvres, serve these with Stuffed Jalapeños (page 132) and Armadillo "Eggs" (page 126).

Found in the Atlantic, north to Cape Cod, there are many varieties of tuna, but the average weight is about 10 pounds. The largest bluefin was 1,496 pounds and caught in Nova Scotia, but the largest tuna on record was a whopping 21 feet long and weighed 1,600 pounds. Tuna is packed with omega-3s, so eating two or three servings per week can improve your cardiac health.

PEPPERCORN TUNA STEAKS

SERVES 2 TO 4 | **250°F** | **APPLE, CHERRY, OR OAK**

BRINING TIME: 8 hours or overnight

PREP TIME: 10 minutes

SMOKE TIME: 1 hour

¼ cup salt

2 pounds yellowfin tuna

¼ cup Dijon mustard

Freshly ground black pepper

2 tablespoons peppercorns

1. In a container large enough to hold the brine and tuna, dissolve the salt in just enough warm water to cover the fish.

2. Place the tuna in the brine, cover, and refrigerate for 8 hours or overnight.

3. Preheat the smoker to 250°F with the apple, cherry, or oak wood.

4. Remove the tuna from the brine and pat dry. Do not rinse the tuna. Place it on a grill pan.

5. Spread the Dijon mustard all over the tuna, season with pepper, and sprinkle with the peppercorns.

6. Place the tuna in the smoker and smoke for about 1 hour, or until it reaches an internal temperature of 125°F.

INGREDIENT TIP: Tuna is a dry fish and works best as a tuna "steak." A brine helps keep it moist during cooking, but watch it so you don't overcook it.

Found in both the North Atlantic and North Pacific, halibut is the world's largest flatfish, and in the flounder family. Why smoke a flatfish? Oh, just for the halibut.

SMOKED HALIBUT

SERVES 4 | **200°F** | **ALDER, APPLE, CHERRY, OR OAK**

MARINATING TIME: 4 to 6 hours

PREP TIME: 15 minutes

SMOKE TIME: 2 hours

½ cup salt

½ cup brown sugar

1 teaspoon smoked paprika

1 teaspoon ground cumin

1 (2-pound) halibut

⅓ cup mayonnaise

1. In a small bowl, mix together the salt, brown sugar, paprika, and cumin. Coat the halibut evenly. Cover and refrigerate for 4 to 6 hours.

2. Preheat the smoker to 200°F with the alder, apple, cherry, or oak wood for a light smoky flavor.

3. Remove the fish from the refrigerator. Rinse it and pat it dry.

4. Rub the mayonnaise on the fish.

5. Place the halibut on a smoker rack and smoke for about 2 hours until the internal temperature reaches 120°F.

INGREDIENT TIP: Halibut is a low-fat fish, which makes it difficult to grill. Marinating first and smoking over low heat while coated in mayonnaise helps solve that problem—but be careful not to overcook it.

Cajun is a rustic French style of cooking out of Louisiana. A true Cajun meal consists of three pots: one with the entrée; one with steamed rice, specially prepared sausages, and/or seafood; and the third, a vegetable. It's generally spicy— think cayenne and lots of black pepper.

COUNTRY CAJUN CATFISH

SERVES 2 TO 4 | **200°F** | **ALDER, APPLE, CHERRY, OR OAK**

BRINING TIME: 4 hours
PREP TIME: 10 minutes
SMOKE TIME: 2 to 2½ hours

1 cup salt

4 to 6 catfish fillets

2 tablespoons Cajun seasoning

2 teaspoons freshly ground black pepper

2 teaspoons ground nutmeg

1 teaspoon ground allspice

¼ cup sriracha

Tartar sauce, for serving

1. In a shallow dish, make a simple brine by dissolving the salt in just enough water to cover the fish. This will help keep the fish from drying out during the smoking process. Submerge the catfish, cover the dish, and refrigerate for at least 4 hours.

2. Preheat the smoker to 200°F with the alder, apple, cherry, or oak wood.

3. Remove the fish from the brine. Rinse it, pat it dry, and discard the liquid.

4. In a small bowl, stir together the Cajun seasoning, pepper, nutmeg, and allspice. Sprinkle this on both sides of the fish.

5. Drizzle with the Sriracha.

6. Place the fish on the smoker grate and smoke for 2 to 2½ hours until the internal temperature reaches 145°F.

7. Serve with tartar sauce.

PREPARATION TIP: Most Southerners like their catfish dredged in cornmeal and pan- or deep-fried, but it is good grilled, baked, or smoked, too.

Buttermilk and bass? The secret ingredient here is, indeed, the buttermilk. The buttermilk-sugar brine for this recipe adds flavor and helps keep the fish from drying out.

SUGARED SEA BASS

SERVES 6 TO 8 | **200°F** | **ALDER OR OAK**

BRINING TIME: Overnight
PREP TIME: 10 minutes
SMOKE TIME: 2½ to 3 hours

4 cups buttermilk

½ cup granulated sugar

¼ cup salt

2 bay leaves, crumbled

1 tablespoon ground cloves

2 teaspoons dried thyme

2 teaspoons dried basil

1½ teaspoons freshly ground black pepper

8 to 10 head-on sea bass

½ cup firmly packed brown sugar

1 lemon, thinly sliced

¼ cup chopped fresh parsley leaves

1. In a large bowl, combine the buttermilk, granulated sugar, salt, bay leaves, cloves, thyme, basil, and pepper to make a brine. Transfer to a container large enough to hold the brine and bass, or divide among multiple containers. Submerge the bass, cover the container, and refrigerate overnight.

2. Preheat the smoker to 200°F with the alder or oak wood.

3. Remove the fish and discard the brine.

4. Pat the fish dry and sprinkle it on both sides with the brown sugar.

5. Place the lemon slices on top of the fish. Sprinkle with the parsley. Place the fish in a single layer on a grill pan and into the smoker for 2½ to 3 hours until the internal temperature reaches 140°F.

PAIR IT: Serve with Smoked Cabbage (page 134) or Smoked Spaghetti Squash (page 144).

Few people have experienced the treat of rustic fire-roasted smoked lobster. Adding hardwood smoke to shellfish always beats a dunk in boiling water when it comes to flavor. It's an easy win for your taste buds. Plus, when you smoke and serve beautiful buttery, hot, split, ruby-red lobsters like this, it's also a winning feast for the eyes. Splitting the lobster tails helps the seasoning and the smoke reach the meat and do its magic (see tip).

SMOKED LOBSTER TAILS

SERVES 4 | **225°F** | **ALDER OR OAK**

PREP TIME: 25 minutes

SMOKE TIME: 1 hour

4 tablespoons (½ stick) butter, melted

Juice of 1 lemon

3 teaspoons freshly ground black pepper

3 teaspoons ground white pepper

2 teaspoons red pepper flakes

1 garlic clove, minced

1 tablespoon lemon-pepper seasoning

4 lobster tails, split at the top of the shell

1. Preheat the smoker to 225°F with the alder or oak wood.

2. In a small bowl, stir together the butter, lemon juice, black and white peppers, red pepper flakes, garlic, and lemon-pepper seasoning.

3. Baste the lobster tails with the seasoned butter and place them on a smoker rack. Smoke for about 30 minutes, then baste again. Continue to smoke for about 30 minutes more, or until the internal temperature reaches 130°F to 140°F.

4. Remove from the heat and baste again. You may need to microwave the lemon butter between bastings to keep it hot. Serve the lobster tails warm.

PREPARATION TIP: Splitting the lobster-tail shells helps the flesh cook evenly. Grasp the tail with the hard shell up and, using strong kitchen shears, split the shell (and the top of the tail meat) down to just before the last shell segment. Devein and remove any grit as needed.

Did you know lobster shells were once used to make the cores of golf balls? Unfortunately the balls only went 70 percent of the distance a typical golf ball does, so they didn't make the cut. With this recipe you might leave the shells behind but there won't be any meat left—I guarantee.

SCUPPERNONG LOBSTER

SERVES 4 | **225°F** | **ALDER OR OAK**

PREP TIME: 40 minutes

SMOKE TIME: 45 minutes to 1 hour

1 bunch scuppernong grapes (or muscadines)

4 tablespoons butter, melted

1 teaspoon freshly ground black pepper

1 teaspoon sea salt

4 lobster tails, split down the middle on top of the shell

1. In a saucepan over high heat, put the scuppernongs and add enough water to cover them. Bring to a boil and cook for about 5 minutes until the grapes are soft or begin to split. Drain in a fine-mesh strainer, then mash through the strainer into a bowl. You should be left with juice and pulp. Discard the skin and seeds.

2. Stir in the butter, pepper, and salt.

3. Season the tails with the spiced-pulp blend. Reserve any unused pulp to baste during cooking.

4. Preheat the smoker to 225°F with the alder or oak wood.

5. Place the lobster tails in the smoker and smoke for 45 minutes to 1 hour until the internal temperature reaches 130°F to 140°F. Start checking after about 30 minutes, and baste the tails whenever you open the smoker to check them, and again when you remove them from the heat.

INGREDIENT TIP: Fun fact—if you haven't heard of scuppernongs, they are a large variety of the muscadine grape, and are found in the South. It is the state fruit of North Carolina. You can eat them off the vine but they are full of small seeds. That is why we boil them and run them through the sieve. You can make jelly and even a wonderful cake with these little-known grapes.

Oysters may not be the world's most beautiful creatures, but sometimes beauty is on the inside. Oysters are loaded with zinc, which boosts your immune system and sex drive, helps get rid of acne, gives you strong bones, alleviates rashes, makes you feel better, and provides extra energy. Eat up!

SMOKY OYSTERS

MAKES 1 DOZEN OYSTERS | **225°F TO 250°F** | **APPLE, CHERRY, OR OAK**

PREP TIME: 30 to 40 minutes

SMOKE TIME: 15 to 20 minutes

1 dozen raw oysters, shucked, oysters left in the bottom shell, top shell discarded

½ cup (1 stick) butter, at room temperature

¼ cup grated Parmesan cheese

2 garlic cloves, minced

3 tablespoons chopped fresh parsley leaves

2 tablespoons hot sauce

1 teaspoon paprika, or cayenne pepper

1. Heat the smoker to 225°F to 250°F with the apple, cherry, or oak wood.

2. Slide a knife under each oyster to loosen it.

3. In a small bowl, blend the butter, Parmesan, garlic, parsley, hot sauce, and paprika. Top each oyster with 1 tablespoon of the butter mixture. Place the oysters in the smoker and smoke for 15 to 20 minutes. Serve immediately.

INGREDIENT TIP: Remember the optimal oyster months by talking like a pirate—Rrrrrrrrrrrr. Oysters are in peak season during the months that have the letter "r" in their names.

With all the talk today about "clean" and healthy eating, shrimp and scallops fit right in. Both are an excellent source of protein and vitamin B_{12}, and shrimp are high in iron, so make some room in your diet for these succulent nibbles. Plus, smoke is low in fat!

SMOKED SHRIMP AND SCALLOPS

SERVES 3 OR 4 | 200°F | CHERRY, MESQUITE, OAK, OR PECAN

PREP TIME: 15 minutes

SMOKE TIME: 25 minutes

½ cup granulated sugar

¼ cup firmly packed brown sugar

2 garlic cloves, finely minced

1 tablespoon hot chili powder

1 tablespoon salt

2 teaspoons ground coriander

2 teaspoons freshly ground black pepper

1 teaspoon ground white pepper

1 teaspoon cayenne pepper

1 teaspoon ground ginger

1 pound jumbo shrimp, peeled, deveined, and tails removed

1 pound sea scallops

Cocktail sauce, lemon wedges, and saltine crackers, for serving

1. Preheat the smoker to 200°F with the cherry, mesquite, oak, or pecan wood.

2. In a small bowl, mix together the granulated sugar, brown sugar, garlic, chili powder, salt, coriander, black pepper, white pepper, cayenne, and ginger to make a rub.

3. Place the shrimp in a large bowl and the scallops in a separate bowl (or use gallon-size resealable plastic bags).

4. Pour half the rub over the shrimp and half over the scallops. Using your hands, make sure everything is well coated.

5. The scallops will take a little longer to cook so place them on a grill pan in a single layer and into the smoker for about 10 minutes.

6. Add the shrimp to the smoker and continue to smoke everything for 15 more minutes.

7. Remove from the heat and serve with cocktail sauce, lemon wedges, and crackers.

PREPARATION TIP: To ease cleanup, use a shallow aluminum foil pan to cook the seafood, which will still take on the smoke flavor.

INGREDIENT TIP: To stir up a quick homemade cocktail sauce, start with ½ cup Heinz chili sauce and add 2 tablespoons prepared horseradish, 1 teaspoon freshly squeezed lemon juice, and a dash of Worcestershire sauce.

Scallops are a great source of vitamin B_{12} and protein, and very low in fat, but watch your portion size as they are high in cholesterol. You can use wet-packed scallops, but I recommend dry-packed because they are usually better quality (see tip).

CITRUS AND GARLIC SCALLOPS

SERVES 3 OR 4 | **200°F** | **CHERRY**

PREP TIME: 10 minutes

SMOKE TIME: 30 to 40 minutes

2 to 3 pounds fresh scallops

1 tablespoon freshly squeezed lemon juice

1 tablespoon freshly squeezed orange juice

1 tablespoon freshly ground black pepper

2 teaspoons salt

1 garlic clove, minced

Zest of 1 orange, lemon, or lime

1. Preheat the smoker to 200°F with the cherrywood.

2. In a large bowl, gently stir the scallops with the lemon and orange juices.

3. Season with the pepper, salt, and garlic. Place the scallops on a grill pan or on skewers and put them into the smoker. Smoke for 30 to 40 minutes. The scallops will turn translucent. As with most seafood, scallops cook faster than you think, so watch them carefully to avoid overcooking.

4. Sprinkle the zest over the scallops before serving warm.

INGREDIENT TIP: Wet scallops are treated with sodium tripolyphosphate (STP), which is a soapy chemical that causes them to retain water and, therefore, release that water during cooking. If you don't watch out, they become rubbery while you wait for them to sear. They are safe to consume, but hard to cook. I recommend using dry-packed scallops if you can get them.

If you are a shrimp fan you are in good company. Year after year shrimp continues to be the most popular seafood in the United States. Being from the Lowcountry (that's the low-lying coastal area of South Carolina), I see shrimp trawlers hard at work on a daily basis. I give you permission to opt for Atlantic- and South Carolina–grown shrimp in this dish. You'll still enjoy plenty of Cajun-inspired heat. Have a cold beer ready. It's important to use mesquite or pecan in this recipe—since the shrimp cook fast, you'll need a wood that will give them flavor quickly.

CAJUN SHRIMP

SERVES 3 OR 4 | **175°F TO 185°F** | **MESQUITE OR PECAN**

PREP TIME: 15 minutes
SMOKE TIME: 15 to 30 minutes

2 to 3 pounds fresh shrimp, peeled and deveined (tails on)

½ cup (1 stick) butter, melted, divided

¼ cup Cajun seasoning

1 heaping tablespoon cayenne pepper

2 teaspoons dried rosemary

French bread, for serving

1. Preheat the smoker to 175°F to 185°F with the mesquite or pecan wood.

2. In a large bowl, toss the shrimp with ¼ cup of melted butter and the Cajun seasoning, cayenne, and rosemary.

3. Pour the remaining ¼ cup of melted butter into an aluminum-foil baking pan with high sides.

4. Lay the shrimp flat in the pan of butter. Place the foil pan on the smoker grate and smoke for about 10 minutes per pound until pink—but watch them, checking every few minutes. They're done when they are fully pink. Do not overcook or the shrimp could get rubbery. (You can also smoke shrimp on kebab skewers.)

5. Serve with torn bread to soak up the heat because these babies are *spicy*!

INGREDIENT TIP: Shrimp size is measured by how many it takes to make a pound. For this recipe, look for medium, or 36 to 50 count.

Shrimp are good grilled, blackened, sautéed, fried, or boiled, and they cook fast no matter how you prepare them. Like Forrest Gump's pal Bubba once said, "Shrimp is the fruit of the sea." In this recipe the crab and bacon elevate the shrimp to the next level.

BACON-WRAPPED CRAB-STUFFED SHRIMP

MAKES 1 DOZEN | **200°F** | **MESQUITE OR PECAN**

PREP TIME: 35 minutes

SMOKE TIME: 20 to 30 minutes

2 cups panko bread crumbs

½ cup (1 stick) butter, melted

1 small onion, finely chopped

Juice of 1 lemon

1 teaspoon salt

1 teaspoon freshly ground black pepper

2 (6-ounce) cans precooked lump crabmeat

1 dozen jumbo shrimp, peeled and deveined (tails on), butterflied

1 pound bacon

1. Preheat the smoker to 200°F with mesquite or pecan wood.

2. In a small bowl, stir together the bread crumbs, butter, onion, lemon juice, salt, pepper, and crabmeat. Using a large melon baller, scoop some of the mixture and place it in the center of each shrimp.

3. Wrap each stuffed shrimp with 1 bacon slice and secure the ends as tightly as possible, tucking them in. Place the shrimp on a grill pan and head to the smoker.

4. Place the shrimp in the smoker and smoke for 20 to 30 minutes until the shrimp are tender and pink.

PAIR IT: For great complementing flavors, serve these with Cajun Alligator Appetizer (page 115) and Smoked Peach Parfait (page 121).

Crabs live in more places than any other animal in the sea; in fact, they are found almost everywhere in the ocean. In South Carolina we have blue crabs, but there are actually more than five thousand species of crab in the world.

CRAB-STUFFED TOMATO

MAKES 8 TOMATOES | **200°F** | **OAK**

PREP TIME: 20 minutes

SMOKE TIME: 45 minutes

1 pound fresh lump crabmeat

2 cups panko bread crumbs

1 cup chopped scallions, white and green parts

2 large eggs, beaten

½ cup (1 stick) butter, melted

¼ cup freshly squeezed lemon juice

1 teaspoon salt

½ teaspoon freshly ground black pepper

8 large tomatoes, hollowed out, leaving enough flesh all around and on the bottom to form a shell

1. Preheat the smoker to 200°F with the oak wood (which I recommend for both tomato and crab).

2. In a large bowl, stir together the crabmeat, bread crumbs, scallions, eggs, butter, lemon juice, salt, and pepper.

3. Stuff the tomatoes with the crab mixture and place them on a grill pan. Place the pan in the smoker and smoke for about 45 minutes.

INGREDIENT TIP: Crabs need to be fresh, so pick up some chicken necks for bait, grab a net, and go crabbing at high tide. You'll have all you need. The rule in our house was you couldn't eat it unless you helped pick the meat out of the shell. It's a tedious process, but definitely worth it!

Smoked Peach Parfait, page 121

113 Smoked Seasoned Duck

114 Smoked Venison Steaks

115 Cajun Alligator Appetizer

116 Pineapple Pigtail

117 Smoked Stuffed
Pumpkin Squash

118 Porchetta Italian Pork
Belly Roast

119 Breakfast Fatty

120 Stuffed Cornish
Game Hens

121 Smoked Peach Parfait

122 Smoked Chorizo-
Stuffed Peppers

123 Rack of Lamb

124 Baba Ghanouj

125 Smoked Bologna

126 Armadillo "Eggs"

127 Big Fat Greek Fatty

SEVEN

NOT YOUR EVERYDAY BARBECUE

Sometimes you have to think outside the smoker box. In the United States we like to stick to the same ol' definition of barbecue. But there is a whole other world beyond brisket, butts, and chicken. If you really want to get people talking, branch out into meats beyond the norm. If you're an avid hunter, venison or duck may not be too unusual, but to many, it's an exotic treat. Gator, game hens, and bologna can be tasty conversation starters, too.

Remember that although you're going for something different, you shouldn't shock your dinner guests. Stick with your usual clean, neat, and eye-pleasing presentation.

TIPS

Keep the following tips in mind for best success:

- Lean meat calls for marinades and moisture.

- Think local. Head to your local farmers' market and ask around to find locally grown vegetables or a special breed of pork and beef to try in your smoker. Eggplant can lead to an unusual Baba Ghanouj (page 124), and a local breed of hog may be a perfect reason to try a pork-belly roast, like the Porchetta Italian Pork Belly Roast (page 118).

- Certain animals won't be helped by smoke. Avoid sea ducks and fowl you might suspect are fish eaters.

- Never smoke unplucked fowl.

- To minimize gamey flavors in wild meats, remove all fat and silverskin, eliminate excess blood, and soak the meat overnight in buttermilk.

Often people think of Sichuan, or Szechuan, cuisine when they think of smoked duck, as the Sichuan province in China is famous for the mouthwatering feast of duck smoked in teak leaves and twigs from the camphor plant. One thing is certain; it is definitely different than chicken.

SMOKED SEASONED DUCK

SERVES 4 | **225°F** | **CHERRY OR PEACH**

PREP TIME: 25 minutes

SMOKE TIME: 3½ to 4 hours

1 (5-pound) whole duck

¾ cup soy sauce

¾ cup honey

¾ cup red table wine

2 tablespoons freshly ground black pepper

1½ tablespoons garlic powder

1. Preheat the smoker to 225°F with the cherry or peach wood.

2. Pierce the skin of the duck with a fork (or tip of a pin) all over the surface of the duck, especially over the fatty areas to aid in rendering the fat out. Use caution NOT to pierce too deeply and hit the meat. This will help crisp the skin (tricky with lower temperatures).

3. In a small bowl, stir together the soy sauce, honey, wine, pepper, and garlic powder. Season the duck inside the cavity and outside on the skin with the mixture. Reserve some liquid for basting later. Put the duck on the grates, breast-side down. Smoke for 2 hours.

4. After the first 2 hours, baste the top of the duck twice, about every hour. The entire smoking time will take 3½ to 4 hours depending on the temperature of your smoker. Cook the duck until the internal breast temperature reaches 165°F.

5. For crisp skin you'll need to enlist the help of high heat for the final 15 minutes. Move the duck to your grill, or even your oven, preheated to 500°F. Many electric smokers cannot achieve high temperatures.

INGREDIENT TIP: Remove as much of the fat in the cavity and around the neck of the duck as possible. Reserve this and render it for that coveted duck fat for cooking (think duck-fat fries) at a later time.

Venison is delicious when smoked, and there are plenty of options when it comes to cuts. You can smoke venison tenderloin, roast, sausages, and even jerky. But if you are in the mood for a good steak, this recipe will have you begging for second helpings.

SMOKED VENISON STEAKS

SERVES 8 | **225°F** | **HICKORY**

MARINATING TIME: 4 to 8 hours

PREP TIME: 10 minutes

SMOKE TIME: 1 hour per pound

1 cup canola oil

2 tablespoons dried oregano

1 tablespoon garlic powder

1 tablespoon dry minced onion

1 tablespoon sugar

1 tablespoon Lawry's seasoned salt

1 tablespoon dried basil

1 tablespoon dried parsley

1 teaspoon freshly ground black pepper

¼ teaspoon dried thyme

¼ teaspoon celery seed

8 venison steaks

1. In a small bowl, whisk together the oil, oregano, garlic powder, onion, sugar, seasoned salt, basil, parsley, pepper, thyme, and celery seed. Place the steaks in a large shallow container and pour the marinade over the steaks. Cover and refrigerate for 4 to 8 hours.

2. Preheat the smoker to 225°F with the hickory wood.

3. Remove the steaks from the marinade and place them directly on the grill grate. Smoke for about 1 hour per pound (based on the weight of the individual steaks) until the internal temperature reaches 160°F.

PREPARATION TIP: For tenderizing tougher cuts of meat, use a meat mallet to break up the fibers and get them ready to absorb a marinade. Cover with heavy-duty plastic wrap before pounding to avoid the mess.

I make my home in the Lowcountry of South Carolina, where I've always loved the wildlife. Egrets, heron, and alligators are plentiful, big, and beautiful. It's hard to believe that alligators were on the brink of extinction and on the endangered species list in the 1960s and '70s. I remember the Wildlife Service removing them from the list in 1987. It was quite the point of conversation on Hilton Head Island golf courses where gators are the rule, not the exception. Although alligator numbers have fully recovered, hunting is regulated and gator farming has become a million-dollar industry.

CAJUN ALLIGATOR APPETIZER

SERVES 8 TO 12 | **225°F** | **MESQUITE**

BRINING TIME: Overnight
PREP TIME: 20 minutes
SMOKE TIME: 2 hours

FOR THE ALLIGATOR

½ gallon water

½ cup Worcestershire sauce

½ cup olive oil

½ cup white wine vinegar

¼ cup salt

¼ cup sugar

1 teaspoon red pepper flakes

2 pounds alligator meat

2 tablespoons Cajun seasoning

FOR THE BUFFALO SAUCE

½ cup (1 stick) butter, melted

½ cup hot sauce

1 teaspoon garlic powder

TO MAKE THE ALLIGATOR

1. In a large bowl, stir together the water, Worcestershire sauce, olive oil, vinegar, salt, sugar, and red pepper flakes, stirring to dissolve the salt and sugar.

2. Place the alligator steaks into the brine, cover the bowl, and refrigerate overnight.

3. Preheat the smoker to 225°F with the mesquite wood.

4. Remove the meat from the marinade and pat it dry. Discard the marinade.

5. Spread the Cajun seasoning all over the alligator and place the pieces directly on the grill grate. Smoke for about 2 hours until the internal temperature reaches 165°F.

6. Remove the alligator from the smoker, cut it into chunks, and serve with the buffalo sauce for dipping.

TO MAKE THE BUFFALO SAUCE

While the meat smokes, in a small bowl, stir together the butter, hot sauce, and garlic powder. Set aside until serving.

INGREDIENT TIP: The tenderloin comes from the tail and is the tenderest cut, but it is easy to overcook.

No, we're not smoking actual hog tail here. That's one area I avoid. Instead, this spiral-cut pineapple just looks like a pig's curly tail. When you wrap it in bacon, well, the name fits.

PINEAPPLE PIGTAIL

SERVES 6 TO 8 | **250°F** | **MAPLE**

PREP TIME: 45 minutes

SMOKE TIME: 1 to 1½ hours

2 tablespoons cayenne pepper

2 tablespoons ground cinnamon

1 tablespoon firmly packed brown sugar

1 whole pineapple

1 pound bacon slices

½ cup maple syrup

1. Preheat the smoker to 250°F with the maple wood.

2. In a small bowl, stir together the cayenne, cinnamon, and brown sugar. Set aside.

3. Cut both ends off the pineapple and use a pineapple corer/slicer/peeler tool to core, slice, and peel the pineapple in one quick and easy step (see tip).

4. Tightly wrap the bacon slices around the pineapple spiral, completely covering the pineapple and overlapping the bacon to secure it, without severing the rings from each other. It should be one continuous bacon-wrapped corkscrew.

5. Baste the bacon with the maple syrup and sprinkle with the spice mixture. Place the pineapple on a Frogmats grill mat and put it in the smoker. Smoke for 1 to 1½ hours until the bacon is fully cooked.

6. Slice into rings to serve.

PREPARATION TIP: You can skin and core a whole pineapple and smoke it using the preceding recipe (Google "Swineapple"), but we like the aesthetics and results of the new handheld pineapple corer/slicers that allow for extra smoky surface area.

This is a fun treat in October when pumpkin squash is plentiful. Acorn squash tastes wonderful as well, and is also perfect for stuffing.

SMOKED STUFFED PUMPKIN SQUASH

SERVES 8 | **225°F** | **MAPLE**

PREP TIME: 30 minutes

SMOKE TIME: 1 to 1½ hours

4 pumpkin squash, or acorn squash, halved horizontally, pulp and seeds discarded

3 tablespoons olive oil

Salt

Freshly ground black pepper

8 ounces dry seasoned stuffing mix

½ cup hot water

½ cup (1 stick) butter, melted

1 egg, beaten

½ cup chopped celery

½ cup chopped onion

2 teaspoons chili powder

Spicy mustard, for drizzling

1. Preheat the smoker to 225°F with the maple wood.

2. Lightly drizzle the cut squash halves with the olive oil and sprinkle with salt and pepper.

3. In a medium bowl, stir together the stuffing mix, water, butter, egg, celery, onion, and chili powder. Stuff the mixture into the squash halves and place the squash directly on the rack inside the smoker. Smoke the stuffed squash for 1 to 1½ hours.

4. Drizzle with spicy mustard and serve warm.

INGREDIENT TIP: Shop for small but heavier squash with dull skin (unless waxed for appearance).

A true porchetta is a large, boneless suckling pig rolled in spices and roasted with wood. It's a little less daunting to use pork belly and tenderloin.

PORCHETTA ITALIAN PORK BELLY ROAST

SERVES 4 TO 6 | 225°F | HICKORY

BRINING TIME: 6 hours
PREP TIME: 30 minutes
SMOKE TIME: 4 to 6 hours

FOR THE RUB

¼ cup firmly packed brown sugar

¼ cup Cajun seasoning

¼ cup fennel seed

¼ cup dried oregano

2 tablespoons salt

2 tablespoons garlic powder

2 tablespoons dry minced onion

2 teaspoons freshly ground black pepper

FOR THE BRINE

1 gallon water

½ cup firmly packed brown sugar

¼ cup salt

¼ cup Cajun seasoning

1 whole pork tenderloin

1 pork belly

TO MAKE THE RUB

In a small bowl, stir together the brown sugar, Cajun seasoning, fennel seed, oregano, salt, garlic powder, onion, and pepper. Set aside.

TO MAKE THE BRINE

1. In a container large enough to hold the brine, tenderloin, and pork belly, stir together the water, brown sugar, salt, and Cajun seasoning, stirring to dissolve the sugar and salt. Submerge the tenderloin and the pork belly in the brine. Cover and refrigerate for a minimum of 6 hours.

2. Preheat the smoker to 225°F with the hickory wood.

3. Drain the meat and pat it dry with paper towels. Discard the liquid.

4. Season both pieces of meat well on all sides with the rub.

5. Wrap the pork belly around the pork tenderloin. With a sharp knife, score the outside with 2-inch slits. Secure the meat with kitchen twine. Add any remaining rub to the outside of the roast and place it on the smoker rack. Smoke the porchetta for 4 to 6 hours (depending on the weight) until the internal temperature reaches about 150°F.

6. Remove the porchetta from the heat and tent it with aluminum foil. Let it rest for 15 to 20 minutes before serving. The internal temperature needs to reach 160°F. This porchetta is great served alone or sliced for a sandwich.

INGREDIENT TIP: Feel free to substitute any of the spices, but fennel is typically a part of the mix.

The world needs more breakfast recipes for the smoker. This breakfast fatty combines your breakfast favorites in one savory loaf. Filling it may make you want to go back to bed, but when was the last time your oatmeal had a smoke ring?

BREAKFAST FATTY

SERVES 4 TO 6 | 275°F | APPLE OR HICKORY

PREP TIME: 35 minutes

SMOKE TIME: 1½ to 2 hours

FOR THE RUB

¼ cup firmly packed light-brown sugar

2 tablespoons paprika

1¼ teaspoons kosher salt

1 teaspoon cayenne pepper

½ teaspoon garlic powder

½ teaspoon onion powder

¼ teaspoon freshly ground black pepper

FOR THE FATTY

5 large eggs, lightly beaten

1 small onion, chopped

1 small bell pepper (any color), chopped

Salt

Freshly ground black pepper

1 pound bacon slices, well chilled

1 pound ground hot sausage, well chilled

1 cup shredded Cheddar cheese

TO MAKE THE RUB

In a small bowl, stir together the brown sugar, paprika, salt, cayenne, garlic powder, onion powder, and pepper. Set aside.

TO MAKE THE FATTY

1. Preheat the smoker to 275°F with the apple or hickory wood.

2. In a large skillet over medium-low heat, lightly scramble the eggs, incorporating the onion and bell pepper. Season with salt and pepper.

3. On a sheet of parchment paper (or plastic wrap), place 6 bacon slices side by side vertically and weave another 6 pieces through them horizontally in an over-under pattern.

4. Layer the sausage on top of the bacon, spreading it out to the edges.

5. Pour the scrambled-egg mixture evenly over the top of the sausage and top with the Cheddar.

6. Sprinkle a bit of the rub on top of the cheese, but reserve most for the outside of the fatty.

7. Roll the fatty up tightly and secure the ends with bacon. Spread the remaining rub all over the outside of the fatty. Place it into the smoker and smoke for 1½ to 2 hours until the internal temperature reaches 165°F. Look for a reddish crust and an impressive smoke ring.

8. Let the fatty rest for about 10 minutes before slicing and serving.

PREPARATION TIP: Start with chilled sausage and bacon and two sheets of parchment (or plastic wrap). Use one sheet for staging the bacon wrap and another to stage and then roll the sausage and fillings. Lastly, transfer the sausage loaf and place it atop the bacon weave to wrap it.

Cornish game hens sound more exotic than they really are. They're not wild game, but simply a breed of chicken. Sometimes called Rock Cornish, or *poussin*, these "hens" are male or female broiler chickens, less than five weeks old. Although the Cornish game hen sounds like it's been around forever, it was bred first in the 1950s. Fun fact: The late funny man and musician Victor Borge was an early investor and promoter who made the dish common.

STUFFED CORNISH GAME HENS

SERVES 2 | **275°F** | **APPLE OR OLIVE**

PREP TIME: 30 minutes

SMOKE TIME: 2 to 3 hours

2 Cornish game hens

Salt

Freshly ground black pepper

4 tablespoons butter, divided

1 cup quick-cooking seasoned brown rice

1 small onion, coarsely chopped

½ cup freshly squeezed orange juice

½ cup apricot jelly

1. Preheat the smoker to 275°F with the apple or olive wood.

2. Season both birds with salt and pepper, including inside the cavities.

3. In a small saucepan over low heat, melt 2 tablespoons of butter and stir in the rice and onion. Stuff the hens with the rice mixture and secure the legs with kitchen twine.

4. Rinse out the saucepan and put it back over low heat. Melt the remaining 2 tablespoons of butter and stir in the orange juice and apricot jelly until smooth. Baste the hens with some of the jelly glaze.

5. Place the birds in the smoker and smoke for 2 to 3 hours until the internal temperature reaches 170°F.

6. Brush with the remaining jelly to serve.

SMOKING TIP: Here are two ways to keep your hens moist and flavorful: pickles and bacon! Use pickle juice for a brine and a bacon wrap for an automatic basting during the second half of the cook.

Fruit and a smoker go well together. Just like the saying goes,
"If you can cook it in the oven, you can cook it in the smoker."

SMOKED PEACH PARFAIT

MAKES 8 PEACH HALVES | **200°F** | **MAPLE**

PREP TIME: 20 minutes

SMOKE TIME: 35 to 45 minutes

4 barely ripe peaches, halved and pitted

1 tablespoon firmly packed brown sugar

1 pint vanilla ice cream

3 tablespoons honey

1. Preheat the smoker to 200°F with the maple wood.

2. Sprinkle the cut peach halves with the brown sugar. Place them in the smoker, cut-side up. Also use a Frogmat to ease cleanup of sticky drippings. Smoke for 35 to 45 minutes.

3. Transfer the peach halves to dessert plates and top each with a scoop of vanilla ice cream.

4. Drizzle with the honey before serving.

SMOKING TIP: Peaches, strawberries, bananas, apples, pears, and pineapples are excellent choices for smoking fruits.

Chorizo originated in Spain and Portugal and is a method of smoking sausage with dried smoked peppers and paprika, traditionally in natural casings made from intestines.

SMOKED CHORIZO-STUFFED PEPPERS

MAKES 8 STUFFED PEPPERS | **225°F** | **APPLE**

PREP TIME: 10 minutes
SMOKE TIME: 2 hours

3 cups shredded Cheddar cheese, divided

2 pounds ground chorizo sausage, casings removed (or ground hot sausage)

4 poblano peppers, halved lengthwise and seeded

8 bacon slices, uncooked

1. Preheat the smoker to 225°F with the applewood.

2. In a large bowl, combine 2 cups of Cheddar with the sausage. Divide the mixture into eight portions and press one portion into each pepper half.

3. Sprinkle with the remaining 1 cup of Cheddar.

4. Wrap each pepper half with 1 bacon slice, tucking in the edges to secure. Place the peppers in the smoker and smoke for 2 hours, or until the sausage reaches an internal temperature of 165°F. Serve immediately.

INGREDIENT TIP: Chorizo can be used in eggs, on pizza, or anywhere you want a hot-and-spicy sausage. You can even purchase a miniature terra-cotta chorizo burner for cooking whole sausages in alcohol.

A traditional rack of lamb is 16 chops cut perpendicular to the spine. We use an American rack here that is one side of the traditional rack and "Frenched" (some of the meat is removed from the bone end) for an impressive presentation.

RACK OF LAMB

MAKES 7 OR 8 CHOPS | **200°F** | **APPLE, CHERRY, LILAC, OR OAK**

PREP TIME: 20 minutes

SMOKE TIME: 1¼ hours

FOR THE PASTE

½ cup olive oil

½ cup dry mustard

¼ cup hot chili powder

2 tablespoons freshly squeezed lemon juice

2 tablespoons dry minced onion

1 tablespoon smoked paprika

1 tablespoon dried thyme

1 tablespoon Worcestershire sauce

1 teaspoon salt

1 American rack of lamb (7 or 8 chops), membrane along the back of the rack removed

FOR THE MINT SAUCE

¼ cup fresh mint leaves, chopped

¼ cup hot water

2 tablespoons apple cider vinegar

2 tablespoons firmly packed brown sugar

½ teaspoon salt

½ teaspoon freshly ground black pepper

TO MAKE THE PASTE

1. In a small bowl, whisk together the olive oil, mustard, chili powder, lemon juice, onion, paprika, thyme, Worcestershire sauce, and salt. Set aside.

2. Preheat the smoker to 200°F with the apple, cherry, lilac, or oak wood.

3. Rub the paste all over the lamb and place it on the smoker rack. Smoke for 1¼ hours until it reaches an internal temperature of 145°F.

4. Remove the lamb from the heat and let it rest for a few minutes before serving with the mint sauce.

TO MAKE THE MINT SAUCE

While the lamb smokes, in a small bowl, stir together the mint, water, vinegar, brown sugar, salt, and pepper. Set aside until serving.

SERVING TIP: I include the traditional mint sauce for serving in this recipe because it is so widely used; however, I prefer to serve the lamb with a jar of green or red jalapeño jelly.

I recently discovered this treat on our last trip home to Chicago, and we since just can't get enough. I was determined to make my own.

BABA GHANOUJ

SERVES 6 TO 8 | **200°F** | **MAPLE**

PREP TIME: 25 to 30 minutes

SMOKE TIME: 1 to 1½ hours

1 eggplant, halved lengthwise

1 tablespoon olive oil

2½ teaspoons salt, divided

2½ tablespoons tahini

Juice of 1 lemon

1 garlic clove, minced

2 tablespoons chopped fresh parsley leaves

Pita chips, for serving

1. Preheat the smoker to 200°F with the maple wood.

2. Rub the eggplant halves with the olive oil and sprinkle with 2 teaspoons of salt. Place the halves on the smoker rack and smoke for 1 to 1½ hours.

3. Remove the eggplant from the smoker. Peel off and discard the skin.

4. Put the eggplant flesh into a food processor and add the tahini, lemon juice, garlic, and remaining ½ teaspoon of salt. Pulse until well blended. Transfer the mixture to a storage container.

5. Stir in the parsley and refrigerate until serving with pita chips.

INGREDIENT TIP: Tahini is a sesame-seed butter found in the refrigerated produce section at your local grocery store. It must be kept cold, but if you don't want to buy the large container, you could reasonably substitute other nut butters or toasted sesame oil.

I haven't been able to figure out just who came up with this processed-meat specialty but it's a fun adventure in barbecue. Some attribute its origins to Oklahoma and call it "Oklahoma Prime Rib" or "Oklahoma Tenderloin."

SMOKED BOLOGNA

MAKES ABOUT 18 (½-INCH) SLICES | **250°F** | **CHERRY**

PREP TIME: 20 minutes

SMOKE TIME: 1 hour

2 tablespoons chili powder

2 tablespoons firmly packed brown sugar

1 teaspoon ground coriander

1 teaspoon ground nutmeg

1 teaspoon garlic powder

1 (5-pound) all-beef bologna chub

¼ cup prepared yellow mustard

Salt

Freshly ground black pepper

1. Preheat the smoker to 250°F with the cherrywood.

2. In a small bowl, mix the chili powder, brown sugar, coriander, nutmeg, and garlic powder. Set aside.

3. Cut the bologna into ½-inch slices and make a few small cuts around the edges of the slices so they lie flat during the cooking process.

4. Coat both sides of each slice with the mustard and season with salt, pepper, and the spice mix. Place the slices on the smoker rack and smoke for 1 hour.

SMOKING TIP: Many pit masters will smoke the entire chub (love that term) in one piece in the smoker. Others will also score the surface of the whole bologna chub in a deep diamond pattern to add extra surface area to caramelize and soak up additional smoke. It looks amazing. Here, I smoke it in thick slices to allow for maximum smoke absorption.

We would never advise smoking a real armadillo (possum on the half-shell). In fact, in the past, eating armadillo was blamed for the spread of leprosy. No—stick with this pork sausage appetizer that gets its name from the shape of the "egg" and the pepper inside.

ARMADILLO "EGGS"

MAKES 6 "EGGS" | **225°F** | **APPLE**

PREP TIME: 35 to 40 minutes
SMOKE TIME: 2 hours

8 ounces cream cheese, at room temperature

1 cup shredded Cheddar cheese

6 jalapeño peppers, cored and seeded

1 pound seasoned ground sausage

1. Preheat the smoker to 225°F with the applewood.

2. In a medium bowl, stir together the cream cheese and Cheddar. Stuff the peppers with the cheese mixture.

3. Divide the sausage into six portions and wrap each jalapeño with one portion, covering the pepper completely. Place the "eggs" directly on the smoker grate. Smoke for about 2 hours until the sausage reaches an internal temperature of 165°F. Serve immediately.

PREPARATION TIP: Of course you can cut off the ends of the jalapeños and dig down in with a knife to remove the membrane and seeds, but if you're preparing a lot of them, save time and pick up an inexpensive jalapeño corer. It also helps eliminate the danger of burning your eyes after handling the peppers.

If you love the lamb-infused flavors of a gyro, you'll love this smoked "Greek" fatty.

BIG FAT GREEK FATTY

SERVES 4 | **225°F** | **OAK**

PREP TIME: 20 minutes
SMOKE TIME: 2 hours

FOR THE FATTY

1 pound ground lamb

1 pound ground beef

1 cup panko bread crumbs

6 garlic cloves, minced

2 eggs

2 tablespoons sesame seeds

2 tablespoons dried oregano

1 tablespoon
Worcestershire sauce

1½ teaspoons salt

1 teaspoon freshly ground
black pepper

1 cup halved cherry tomatoes,
well drained, plus more
for serving

1 medium red onion, thinly sliced

1 cucumber, seeded, dried and
cut into julienne strips

1 tablespoon chopped fresh
parsley leaves

Pita points, for serving

FOR THE TZATZIKI SAUCE

1 cucumber, seeded, dried and
coarsely chopped

Juice of 1 lemon

3 garlic cloves, minced

2 tablespoons chopped fresh dill

1 cup plain yogurt

½ teaspoon salt

¼ teaspoon freshly ground
black pepper

TO MAKE THE FATTY

1. Preheat the smoker to 225°F with the oak wood.

2. In a large bowl, mix the lamb, beef, bread crumbs, garlic, eggs, sesame seeds, oregano, Worcestershire sauce, salt, and pepper until well blended. On a rimmed baking sheet, roll or press the mixture out flat (about 8 to 10 inches square).

3. Starting on the left side and using half of each ingredient, create a row of cherry tomatoes, a row of red onion, and a row of cucumber. Repeat, leaving a clear space at the end.

4. From the left side, roll the fatty up tightly and place it in the smoker, seam-side down. Smoke for about 2 hours until the meat is cooked to an internal temperature of 145°F.

5. Sprinkle with the parsley. Slice and serve with pita-bread points, halved cherry tomatoes, and tzatziki sauce.

TO MAKE THE TZATZIKI SAUCE

1. While the fatty is smoking, in a medium bowl, stir together the cucumber, lemon juice, garlic, and dill until well blended.

2. Stir in the yogurt, salt, and pepper. Refrigerate until ready to serve.

INGREDIENT TIP: Lamb is a great source of vitamin B_{12} and niacin, but substitute for beef in this dish if you prefer.

Garlic-Rosemary Potato Wedges, page 136

EIGHT

VEGETABLES & SIDES

131 Smoked Coleslaw

132 Stuffed Jalapeños

133 Smoked Onion Bombs

134 Smoked Cabbage

135 Loaded Hasselback
Potatoes

136 Garlic-Rosemary
Potato Wedges

137 Smoked Asparagus

138 Smoked Bacon-Wrapped
Onion Rings

139 Smoked Artichokes

140 Hasselback
Sweet Potatoes

141 Smoked Deviled Eggs

142 Smoked Corn on the Cob

143 Potato Bacon Bites

144 Smoked Spaghetti Squash

145 Smoked Cauliflower
Steaks

Vegetables come in all shapes and sizes. Thankfully, most are shaped and sized to fit nicely inside your smoker. In fact, vegetables offer you a far greater variety of delicious flavors to discover than meats, and the colors can be a dazzling feast for the eyes.

"CUTS"

Vegetables can take longer to prepare for the smoker, but they actually absorb smoke much faster than meat. In short, vegetables are great for the smoker and are a perfect match as a side to your smoked meat, yet strong enough to serve on their own. Root vegetables work really well with this kind of cooking, and the flavor is beyond compare.

TECHNIQUES

As with the other foods discussed, marinating vegetables prior to smoking is a great way to prepare them, as is cooking them in a moist environment. Cut similar vegetables into uniform sizes, shapes, and thickness to allow for even cook times.

FINAL TIPS FOR VEGETABLE BARBECUE SUCCESS

When adding vegetables to your smoker, keep the following in mind for best results:

- Use the water pan. This will keep the moisture level up in the smoking chamber.

- If you're leaving the skin on the vegetable, keep in mind the Environmental Working Group's Dirty Dozen (ewg.org) and consider buying organic. Smoker favorites like peaches, peppers, and potatoes are on the list of most contaminated vegetables.

- Marinades work as well on vegetables as they do on meat—often better. Eggplant and zucchini are two of the best vegetables for absorbing liquid marinades.

- If cooking vegetables along with the main feature, consider their cook time and place them in the smoker accordingly.

- Some vegetables don't require anything but a little salt, pepper, and smoke to taste great. But add a light brushing of olive oil to keep them from sticking to the grates. Or use Frogmats.

Fast-food diners like a lot of sweet in their coleslaw. KFC uses mayonnaise and buttermilk instead of the heavy cream I use in my recipe. Chick-fil-A used mayonnaise and a little dry mustard before discontinuing their popular side. Most coleslaws have a significant amount of sugar, which makes this slaw decidedly different from its vinegar-based cousin. This recipe is adapted from one belonging to a church friend, Fran Bendure, and it's the best I've ever tasted. I just kicked it up a bit by smoking the cabbage and carrot.

SMOKED COLESLAW

SERVES 10 TO 12 | **175°F** | **MAPLE**

MARINATING TIME: 1 hour

PREP TIME: 10 minutes

SMOKE TIME: 30 minutes

1 head cabbage, shredded

1 carrot, shredded

¼ cup sugar

½ teaspoon salt

½ teaspoon freshly ground black pepper

¼ cup white vinegar

1 cup heavy (whipping) cream (do not whip)

1 teaspoon paprika

1. Preheat the smoker to 175°F with the maple wood.

2. Spread the cabbage and carrot in a shallow aluminum foil pan. Place the pan in the smoker and smoke the vegetables for 30 minutes. Remove from the smoker and transfer the vegetables to a large bowl.

3. Stir in the sugar, salt, pepper, vinegar, and heavy cream to combine. Refrigerate for 1 hour before serving.

4. Sprinkle with paprika.

VARIATION TIP: This sweet dressing is also excellent for a broccoli-cauliflower salad. Instead of the cabbage and carrot, use 2 cups each of chopped broccoli, cauliflower, and cooked bacon, and add 1 cup each of chopped scallions (white and green parts) and celery.

Good things come in small packages, but be careful—the size and color of a typical jalapeño pepper never seems to correlate directly to its heat intensity. The jalapeño is the most popular of all hot peppers, so it's only fitting the pepper has its own special dish in which to shine.

STUFFED JALAPEÑOS

MAKES 12 PEPPERS | **250°F** | **MAPLE**

PREP TIME: 20 minutes

SMOKE TIME: 1 to 1½ hours

8 ounces sharp Cheddar cheese, shredded

8 ounces cream cheese, at room temperature

1 tablespoon red pepper flakes

12 jalapeño peppers, sliced lengthwise on one side (not halved), seeded and membranes removed

12 bacon slices

2 teaspoons freshly ground black pepper

1. Preheat the smoker to 250°F with the maple wood.

2. In a large bowl, stir together the Cheddar, cream cheese, and red pepper flakes. Stuff some of the cheese mixture into each jalapeño.

3. Wrap each stuffed pepper with 1 bacon slice and secure it with toothpicks, or tuck the bacon ends in securely.

4. Sprinkle with the black pepper.

5. Place the stuffed jalapeños on a grill pan and put them inside the smoker. Smoke for 1 to 1½ hours until the bacon is cooked. You can speed the process by partially cooking the bacon before wrapping the peppers.

PREPARATION TIP: Use rubber gloves when handling jalapeños and wash your hands thoroughly before touching your eyes or other sensitive body parts.

A single great ingredient can turn a simple recipe into something really outstanding. Such is the case with a quality Vidalia onion. That city in Toombs County, Georgia, was able to take advantage of the low amount of sulfur in the soil there. Now, the name "Vidalia" has been trademarked, and it's no surprise the Vidalia onion is Georgia's official state vegetable. Of course, you can smoke other kinds of onions, and I suggest sticking close to your roots.

SMOKED ONION BOMBS

SERVES 4 | **225°F** | **MAPLE OR MESQUITE**

PREP TIME: 15 minutes
SMOKE TIME: 2 hours

4 large Vidalia onions, peeled
½ cup (1 stick) butter, divided
4 chicken bouillon cubes
½ cup grated Parmesan cheese
1 teaspoon freshly ground black pepper

1. Preheat the smoker to 225°F with the maple or mesquite wood.

2. Angle a sharp knife into the onion from the top and cut all the way around, removing the top and creating a deep well in the onion. Repeat with the remaining onions. Save the onion tops.

3. Tear off four pieces of aluminum foil, each about 8 inches square. Place each onion on a sheet of foil. Press 2 tablespoons of butter into the well of each onion and top with a bouillon cube.

4. In a small bowl, mix the Parmesan and pepper. Put about 2 tablespoons of the mixture in each onion well.

5. Replace the onion tops tightly (cutting as necessary to fit) and wrap the foil up the sides, but leave the top of the packet open to allow the smoke flavor to permeate the onions.

6. Smoke the onions for about 2 hours, until tender.

INGREDIENT TIP: When shopping in the produce section, look for firm bulbs with no bruises or soft areas. Onions can be kept in the refrigerator's crisper drawer, but avoid storing in plastic bags, as the onions are then prone to develop mold.

This is a unique way to prepare cabbage, and oh, so delicious. It's not just for corned beef—this side pairs with any meat.

SMOKED CABBAGE

SERVES 4 | **240°F** | **APPLE, MAPLE, OR OAK**

PREP TIME: 10 minutes

SMOKE TIME: 2 hours

1 head cabbage, cored completely

4 tablespoons butter

2 tablespoons rendered bacon fat, or 2 more tablespoons butter, melted

1 chicken bouillon cube

1 teaspoon freshly ground black pepper

1 garlic clove, minced

1. Preheat the smoker to 240°F with the apple, maple, or oak wood.

2. Fill the hole left by coring the cabbage with the butter, bacon fat, bouillon cube, pepper, and garlic.

3. Wrap the cabbage in aluminum foil, two-thirds of the way up the sides to protect the outer leaves, leaving the top open to allow the smoke flavor to permeate the cabbage. Place the cabbage on the grill rack and smoke for about 2 hours.

4. Unwrap and enjoy as a side dish.

PAIR IT: This is a winner with Plum Chicken Pops (page 50).

The flashy Hasselback potato is a Swedish side dish that gets its name from the restaurant Hasselbacken in Stockholm, where the famed spud was first served.

LOADED HASSELBACK POTATOES

MAKES 4 POTATOES | **250°F** | **HICKORY**

PREP TIME: 20 minutes

SMOKE TIME: 1½ hours

4 russet potatoes, cut Hasselback style (slice into the potato, all the way across, making your cuts about ¼ inch apart and being careful not to cut all the way through the bottom of the potato; see tip, page 140)

1 cup olive oil, divided

2 teaspoons salt

2 teaspoons freshly ground black pepper

1 small onion, sliced

2 jalapeño peppers, seeded and thinly sliced

2 cherry peppers, sliced

4 ounces block Cheddar cheese, thickly sliced

8 bacon slices, cooked and crumbled

1. Preheat the smoker to 250°F with the hickory wood.

2. Place the potatoes on a grill pan. Drizzle ½ cup of olive oil over the potatoes and sprinkle with the salt and pepper. Place the pan in the smoker and smoke for about 1 hour.

3. Remove the potatoes from the smoker and place some onion, jalapeños, cherry peppers, Cheddar slices, and crumbled bacon in between each potato slice and on top.

4. Pour the remaining ½ cup of olive oil over all. Return the potatoes to the smoker for 30 to 40 minutes or so, until the potatoes are tender in a squeeze test.

5. Serve with sour cream, if desired.

INGREDIENT TIP: Replace fancy olive oil with reserved bacon grease. You'll need a bit more than the drippings generated by the eight slices here. After being cooled, the grease spreads nicely in between the potato slices and really packs a rustic flavor punch.

Potatoes absorb smoke better than any other vegetable. Once you experience the robust smokiness of this slow-cooked spud, you'll never go back to cooking potatoes in the oven.

GARLIC-ROSEMARY POTATO WEDGES

SERVES 6 TO 8 | **250°F** | **MAPLE OR PECAN**

PREP TIME: 15 minutes

SMOKE TIME: 1½ hours

4 to 6 large russet potatoes, cut into wedges

¼ cup olive oil

2 garlic cloves, minced

2 tablespoons chopped fresh rosemary leaves, or 1 tablespoon dried rosemary

2 teaspoons salt

1 teaspoon freshly ground black pepper

1 teaspoon sugar

1 teaspoon onion powder

1. Preheat the smoker to 250°F with the maple or pecan wood.

2. In a large bowl, toss the potatoes with the olive oil to coat them well.

3. In a small bowl, stir together the garlic, rosemary, salt, pepper, sugar, and onion powder. Sprinkle this mixture on all sides of the potato wedges. Transfer the seasoned wedges to a grill pan and put it into the smoker.

4. Cook for about 1½ hours until a fork cuts through the wedges easily.

PAIR IT: For a new take on steak and potatoes, serve these with Smoked Tri-Tip Roast (page 76).

Asparagus in the smoker adds an air of sophistication to a summer barbecue. Asparagus is native to coastal areas of Europe, Africa, and Asia and was brought to the United States back in the 1700s. It's considered a superfood for its superior amount of folate, which helps brain function and improves mood. I just think it looks cool coming out of the smoker.

SMOKED ASPARAGUS

SERVES 4 OR 5 | **240°F** | **MAPLE**

PREP TIME: 10 minutes

SMOKE TIME: 1 hour

2 tablespoons butter, melted

2 garlic cloves, minced

2 tablespoons freshly squeezed lemon juice

1 tablespoon capers

1 tablespoon onion powder

1 teaspoon salt

½ teaspoon freshly ground black pepper

1 pound asparagus (about 18 to 20 stalks), woody ends snapped off

1. Preheat the smoker to 240°F with the maple wood.

2. In a small bowl, stir together the butter, garlic, lemon juice, capers, onion powder, salt, and pepper.

3. Place the asparagus in a grill pan and drizzle with the seasoned butter. Put the pan in the smoker and smoke for about 1 hour until tender.

INGREDIENT TIP: You don't need to peel thin asparagus stalks, but sometimes the bottom portion of the stalk can become woody. Peeling the bottom stalk using a vegetable peeler like you would peel a carrot also enhances appearance and tenderness.

This is a heavy-duty onion ring! You'll have better results if you don't try to go too big with the rings. Opt for thin bacon slices and stretch them out as you go to maximize the length of each slice. Bacon won't get crispy in a smoker but will get past the chewy phase and become nicely firm.

SMOKED BACON-WRAPPED ONION RINGS

MAKES 16 ONION RINGS | **250°F** | **HICKORY, MAPLE, OR MESQUITE**

PREP TIME: 20 minutes
SMOKE TIME: 1½ hours

2 large onions, peeled and sliced ½ inch thick (about 4 slices from each onion)

¼ cup hot sauce

4 tablespoons butter, melted

1 pound bacon

1 tablespoon cayenne pepper

1 tablespoon sugar

1. Preheat the smoker to 250°F with the hickory, maple, or mesquite wood.

2. Separate the onion rings and remove the smaller internal rings to save for another use. I recommend leaving two rings intact on each to keep them sturdy. You should get about eight rings out of one large onion, two out of each slice.

3. In a small shallow bowl, mix together the hot sauce and melted butter.

4. Dip the onion rings in the butter–hot sauce mixture.

5. Wrap each onion ring tightly with a bacon slice.

6. In another small bowl, stir together the cayenne and sugar. Coat the bacon-wrapped rings well with this mixture. Secure the rings with toothpicks or place them on skewers.

7. Place the onion rings on a grill mat and smoke for about 1½ hours until the bacon is done and beyond "chewy" to bite through.

PAIR IT: Ditch the plain ketchup and serve these with Carolina Mustard Sauce (page 164) or Plum Sauce (page 172) for dipping.

Artichokes are like asparagus in the sophisticated smoking category but, believe it or not, the artichoke is actually a species of thistle. Don't let that scare you (see tip). The flavor is outstanding and you'll look like a pit-master chef when these emerge from your billowing smoker.

SMOKED ARTICHOKES

SERVES 8 | **225°F** | **HICKORY OR MAPLE**

PREP TIME: 5 minutes

SMOKE TIME: 2 hours

¼ cup olive oil

1 garlic clove, minced

1 teaspoon salt

Juice of 1 lemon

4 artichokes, stemmed and halved lengthwise

1. Preheat the smoker to 225°F with the hickory or maple wood.

2. In a small bowl, whisk together the olive oil, garlic, salt, and lemon juice.

3. Brush the artichoke halves with the seasoned olive oil. Place them directly on the smoker's grate and smoke for about 2 hours. The artichoke bottoms should look and feel tender when poked with a fork.

INGREDIENT TIP: Enjoy the bottom of the petals and don't miss the coveted artichoke heart. However, be sure to discard the hairy-looking choke that covers the heart. Let's just say it's a reminder that you're eating a thistle.

Potatoes of all kinds take well to smoke. In addition,
the tough sweet potato benefits from a long cook time.

HASSELBACK SWEET POTATOES

SERVES 4 TO 6 | **250°F** | **PECAN**

PREP TIME: 15 minutes

SMOKE TIME: 1½ hours

4 large sweet potatoes, scrubbed

¼ cup canola oil

2 tablespoons table salt

½ cup (1 stick) butter

4 serrano peppers, seeded and sliced

1 cup Glazed Spiced Pecans (page 159), coarsely chopped

1 tablespoon sea salt

¼ cup honey

1. Preheat the smoker to 250°F with the pecan wood.

2. Rub the sweet potatoes all over with the oil and table salt.

3. Cut them thick-sliced Hasselback-style: Slice into the sweet potatoes, all the way across, making your cuts about ½ inch apart, and being careful not to cut all the way through the bottom of the sweet potato (see tip).

4. Place the sweet potatoes on a grill pan and put it into the smoker. Smoke for 1 hour, then remove from the heat.

5. Place a pat of butter between each slice.

6. Stuff serrano slices and pecans between the slices.

7. Sprinkle well with the sea salt and drizzle with the honey, getting it between the slices.

8. Smoke for 30 to 40 minutes more and remove from the smoker when the potatoes pass the squeeze test.

PREPARATION TIP: Use caution slicing the hard sweet potatoes. Create a flat bottom by trimming off a thin piece on one long side. Then, align two wooden spoons in parallel on a cutting board with the sweet potato flat-side down and lengthwise in between the spoons. Use the wooden spoons as a stop to create uniform slices without cutting through the sweet potato.

No supper ever has enough deviled eggs. Adding smoke
will only make this more of a dilemma.

SMOKED DEVILED EGGS

MAKES 12 DEVILED EGGS | 200°F | HICKORY

PREP TIME: 10 minutes

SMOKE TIME: 20 to 30 minutes

6 hardboiled eggs, peeled

¼ cup mayonnaise

2 tablespoons sweet pickle–
salad cubes, well drained

1 teaspoon salt

1 teaspoon freshly ground
black pepper

½ teaspoon dry mustard

2 teaspoons paprika

4 pimento-stuffed green olives,
cut into thirds

1. Preheat the smoker to 200°F with the hickory wood.

2. Place the eggs in the smoker and smoke for 20 to 30 minutes.
Remove from the heat.

3. Halve the eggs lengthwise and scoop the cooked yolk into a small
bowl, leaving the egg whites intact.

4. Using a fork, mash the yolks and mix them with the mayonnaise,
pickle cubes, salt, pepper, and mustard.

5. Using a small melon baller, drop the yolk mixture into the egg white
halves and sprinkle each with the paprika.

6. Top each with an olive slice before serving.

PREPARATION TIP: You can get fancy even without a pastry bag
by piping the egg-yolk mixture into the whites via a resealable zipper
bag. Fill the corner of a bag with the filling and cut a small triangle
off the bottom corner of the bag. Squeeze the bag from the top
toward the cut corner to pipe the mixture into the egg whites.

Nothing screams summer cookout like a platter full of beautiful corn on the cob. This summer staple is taken to the highest level with an infusion of maple smoke and a final drench of chipotle butter and cheese.

SMOKED CORN ON THE COB

MAKES 6 TO 8 EARS | **225°F** | **MAPLE**

PREP TIME: 15 minutes

SMOKE TIME: 1½ hours

½ cup mayonnaise

1 tablespoon chili powder

Juice of 1 lime

6 to 8 fresh ears of corn, silk ends removed and discarded, husks peeled back but still attached

½ cup (1 stick) butter

2 chipotle peppers in adobo sauce, diced

1 tablespoon adobo sauce

2 teaspoons salt

1 tablespoon chopped fresh cilantro leaves

½ cup queso fresco cheese, crumbled, or Parmesan or Asiago or Romano

1. Preheat the smoker to 225°F with the maple wood.

2. In a small bowl, whisk together the mayonnaise, chili powder, and lime juice. Slather the mayo mixture on each corncob and carefully pull the husks back up around the cob. Secure with kitchen twine. Place the corn in the smoker and smoke for 1½ hours.

3. While the corn smokes, in a small saucepan over medium heat, melt the butter.

4. Stir in the chipotles, adobo sauce, and salt. Mix well and heat through.

5. Pull down the husks for presentation or remove them completely. Pour the chipotle sauce over the corn and sprinkle with the cilantro and cheese.

INGREDIENT TIP: May through July is the best time for fresh corn. Look for Silver Queen (white) corn, which is the sweetest.

Potato skins are the ultimate tailgate food. Hearty and hand-held. This smokified version uses bite-size potatoes to create a mini version of the classic. Bet you can't stop at just one.

POTATO BACON BITES

SERVES 5 OR 6 | **250°F** | **HICKORY**

PREP TIME: 15 minutes

SMOKE TIME: 1½ hours

6 small red potatoes, or baby Dutch yellow potatoes

¾ cup (1½ sticks) butter, cut into 12 (tablespoon-size) slices

1 tablespoon chili powder

1 tablespoon garlic powder

2 teaspoons salt

2 teaspoons freshly ground black pepper

8 bacon slices, cooked and crumbled

½ cup chopped scallions, white and green parts

1 cup shredded Cheddar cheese

1 tablespoon dried parsley

Sour cream, for serving

1. Prick the potatoes with a fork and microwave on high power for 2 to 3 minutes. They should still be firm. Remove and let them cool.

2. Halve the cooled potatoes and scoop out the centers, leaving enough potato to keep the sides and bottom intact. Discard the extra potato or save for another use.

3. Place a pat of butter in the center of each potato shell.

4. In a small bowl, stir together the chili powder, garlic powder, salt, pepper, bacon, and scallion. Top each potato with some of this mixture and sprinkle on the Cheddar. Place the potatoes on a smoker rack and smoke for about 1½ hours until tender.

5. Sprinkle with the parsley and serve with sour cream.

PAIR IT: Make it a real party and serve with Cinnamon-Cured Fire-Smoked Chicken (page 47).

Spaghetti squash has risen in popularity over the years as a low-carb substitute for pasta. With the addition of smoke, the squash "noodles" are delicious as they are or topped like pasta.

SMOKED SPAGHETTI SQUASH

SERVES 4 | **275°F** | **CHERRY OR MAPLE**

PREP TIME: 10 minutes

SMOKE TIME: 2½ to 3 hours

1 spaghetti squash, ends trimmed, halved lengthwise, seeds and pulp discarded

2 tablespoons olive oil

2 teaspoons salt

2 teaspoons freshly ground black pepper

1. Preheat the smoker to 275°F with the cherry or maple wood.

2. Rub the cut sides of the squash generously with the olive oil and sprinkle with the salt and pepper. Place the squash, cut-sides down, on a grill pan and smoke for 2½ to 3 hours until the flesh pulls apart into strands easily.

3. Discard the skins and serve the squash as a side dish, or use in place of pasta with marinara or Alfredo sauce.

PREPARATION TIP: Microwave the whole spaghetti squash for 2 to 3 minutes on high power to soften it just enough to make it easier to cut through.

Cauliflower has become the darling of food bloggers due to its ability to transform itself into various shapes and sizes. It also absorbs all sorts of flavors. I love using it as a low-carb pizza crust and mock garlic mashed "potatoes." But for smoking and grilling, I love using it as a steak that absorbs marinades as easily as it absorbs smoke flavor.

SMOKED CAULIFLOWER STEAKS

SERVES 4 | **250°F** | **MAPLE**

MARINATING TIME: 10 minutes

PREP TIME: 10 minutes

SMOKE TIME: 45 minutes to 1 hour

2 heads cauliflower, leaves removed

¼ cup olive oil

¼ cup A1 Sauce, or Heinz 57 Steak Sauce, plus more for serving

2 garlic cloves, minced

2 teaspoons salt

2 teaspoons freshly ground black pepper

1. Preheat the smoker to 250°F with the maple wood.

2. Trim the base off each cauliflower. Save the excess cauliflower florets for another use.

3. Carefully slice each head of cauliflower from top to bottom through the base into 2 thick slices.

4. In a small bowl, stir together the olive oil, steak sauce, garlic, salt and pepper. Brush both sides of the "steaks" with the mixture and let them marinate on the counter for about 10 minutes to absorb the flavors.

5. Place the cauliflower directly on a grill rack. Smoke for 45 minutes to 1 hour until tender.

6. Serve with additional steak sauce.

PREPARATION TIP: Try the same slicing technique using cabbage, and even broccoli, for other unique vegetarian "steaks."

Barbecue Almonds and Cashews, page 158

NINE

CHEESE & NUTS

149 Smoked Mac and Cheese

150 Spicy Piggy Mac

151 Smoked Brie with Brown Sugar and Pecans

152 Smoked Cheesecake

153 Cold-Smoked Cheeses

154 Hot-Smoked Gouda Bacon Dip

155 Smoked Tomato-Mozzarella Dip

156 Spicy Smoky Snack Mix

157 Smokehouse Almonds

158 Barbecue Almonds and Cashews

159 Glazed Spiced Pecans

Cheese and nuts are the perfect partners for smoke and salt. You can't eat just one. Not even just one handful. I struggle with stopping at one bowlful! At least this is a way to keep your snack food all natural: You don't need added preservatives because there won't be anything left over.

"CUTS"

To get the most "smoke" out of smoking nuts and cheeses, think small. Using smaller cuts or pieces provides more surface area to absorb those tasty smoky flavors.

TECHNIQUES

Nuts are fairly straightforward—just use your typical low-and-slow smoking. Cheese, however, can be a little trickier. There are a few special ways to treat this dairy product.

You can smoke most cheeses for as long as they stay firm enough not to fall through the grates of your electric smoker. However, to smoke cheese correctly you need to employ a trick called "cold-smoking." You want only the smoke and *not* the heat from the heating element inside your electric smoker.

FINAL TIPS FOR CHEESE AND NUT BARBECUE SUCCESS

For the best results, keep the following key tips in mind when smoking cheeses (especially) and nuts:

- **Be cool.** Cold-smoking allows you to add smoky flavor without melting, cooking, or degrading the structure of the cheese. Your electric smoker may require a cold-smoking kit. Bradley and Masterbuilt offer cold-smoke units that are sold separately. Other smokers, such as Char-Broil's Deluxe XL, can only be set as low as 100°F. There are hacks on YouTube about using pans of ice and trying it in the winter, but cold smoking is not recommended without a cold-smoking kit or in a smoker that cannot be set to a temperature lower than 90°F.

- **Size matters.** You will get better results using smaller pieces because, overall, you end up with more smoky surface area.

- **No sweat.** Start with room-temperature cheese. Chilled cheese may sweat. Blot and dry the cheese while it adjusts to room temperature. This will help develop better skin.

- **Let it rest.** Just like meat, cheese needs to pause after smoking. A minimum rest of 24 hours, and up to 1 week in the refrigerator, lets the flavors mellow and improve.

- **Low and slow.** You want the smoker to sustain a temperature lower than 90°F. You may, indeed, need to wait for cold weather to smoke cheese.

Here in the South we *love* our mac and cheese. In Charleston, South Carolina, we even have an annual Mac Off competition. There is an ongoing argument over whether traditional mac and cheese should be baked, contain eggs, be made with a roux, etc. In this recipe I encourage you to experiment by replacing or substituting any of the ingredients *except* three: mac, cheese, and smoke.

SMOKED MAC AND CHEESE

SERVES 8 | **225°F** | **HICKORY OR MESQUITE**

PREP TIME: 25 minutes

SMOKE TIME: 1 hour

4 tablespoons butter

3 tablespoons all-purpose flour

3 cups whole milk

2 cups shredded sharp Cheddar cheese, divided

2 cups shredded Monterey Jack cheese

1 cup grated Parmesan cheese, or Asiago or Roman

8 ounces cream cheese, cubed

2 teaspoons salt

1 teaspoon freshly ground black pepper

1 pound elbow macaroni, cooked according to package directions, drained

Nonstick cooking spray

1. Preheat the smoker to 225°F with the hickory or mesquite wood.

2. In a large saucepan over medium heat, melt the butter.

3. Whisk in the flour, continuing to whisk for about 1 minute until the flour is well incorporated.

4. Slowly whisk in the milk and bring to a boil. Reduce the heat to low and cook for 5 minutes until thickened. Remove from the heat.

5. Add 1½ cups of Cheddar, the Monterey Jack, Parmesan, and cream cheese. Stir the sauce until the cheeses melt.

6. Stir in the salt, pepper, and cooked macaroni.

7. Spray a half-size steam-table aluminum-foil roasting pan with nonstick cooking spray. Transfer the mac and cheese to the prepared pan and top with the remaining ½ cup of Cheddar cheese.

8. Place the pan in the smoker and smoke for about 1 hour until the cheese is bubbly.

PAIR IT: This traditional barbecue side is the ultimate partner for Simple Smoked Pork Shoulder (page 67).

What to do with leftover barbecue? This is an excellent side dish to serve with ribs, or it can stand alone as a meal in itself!

SPICY PIGGY MAC

SERVES 8 TO 12 | **275°F** | **HICKORY OR MESQUITE**

PREP TIME: 20 minutes

SMOKE TIME: 1 hour

16 ounces elbow macaroni, cooked according to package directions

2 cups heavy whipping cream

8 ounces cream cheese, softened

1 teaspoon salt

1 teaspoon pepper

2 tablespoons Bisquick mix

½ cup panko bread crumbs

8 slices bacon, cooked and crumbled

½ cup coarsely chopped red onion

1 jalapeño pepper, seeded and finely chopped

2 cups Simple Smoked Pork Shoulder (page 67)

1 cup Spicy Hickory-Smoked Barbecue Sauce (page 163)

4 cups shredded sharp Cheddar cheese, divided

1. Preheat smoker to 275°F and add hickory or mesquite woodchips.

2. Place the hot, cooked pasta in a shallow metal, nonstick baking pan.

3. Add in the whipping cream, cream cheese, salt, pepper, Bisquick mix, breadcrumbs, bacon, red onion, jalapeño, smoked pork shoulders, spicy sauce, and 2 cups of Cheddar, and stir until fully incorporated.

4. Top with the remaining Cheddar.

5. Place the pan in the preheated smoker and smoke for about 1 hour, until it's bubbly and the cheese is melted.

PAIR IT: Try it with Competition Baby Back Ribs (page 58).

Brie is a soft cow's-milk cheese from France. It has a soft, edible rind, although I cut the top rind off for this recipe so the cheese absorbs more smoke. I recommend leaving the rind on the bottom and sides as this is a melty cheese.

SMOKED BRIE WITH BROWN SUGAR AND PECANS

SERVES 8 TO 10 | **175°F TO 200°F** | **APPLE OR CHERRY**

PREP TIME: 5 minutes

SMOKE TIME: 20 to 30 minutes

1 (16-ounce) Brie wheel, rind intact

½ cup firmly packed brown sugar

1 teaspoon ground cinnamon

½ cup chopped Glazed Spiced Pecans (page 159), divided

Crackers or pear and Granny Smith apple wedges, for serving

1. Preheat the smoker to 200°F with the apple or cherrywood.

2. Place the whole Brie wheel on a piece of aluminum foil. Bring the foil up the sides but leave the top of the Brie uncovered. Place the foil-wrapped Brie in a metal or foil pie pan. Carefully cut off the rind from the top of the Brie only, leaving a ¼-inch border intact.

3. Cover the top of the cheese with the brown sugar and sprinkle with the cinnamon and ¼ cup of pecans.

4. Place the pan on the top rack of the smoker and smoke for 20 to 30 minutes. Remove when the cheese is melty, and top with the remaining ¼ cup of pecans.

5. Serve warm with crackers or pear and apple wedges.

SMOKING TIP: You can smoke Brie on a cedar plank and top it with jam or other sweet, or even savory, ingredients. The possibilities are endless. Just lower the smoke temperature to 175°F or lower if you don't have it wrapped in foil or in a pan. Melted cheese through the grates of your smoker will not be fun to clean.

Cheesecake can be traced to ancient Greece and Rome, although I doubt it was slow-smoked. This version is all-American, and the basic recipe is adapted from one by my brother-in-law Paul Stewart, who is a chef/restaurant owner on Hilton Head Island.

SMOKED CHEESECAKE

SERVES 14 TO 16 | **275°F** | **APPLE, CHERRY, OR PEACH**

REFRIGERATION TIME: 4 hours

PREP TIME: 15 minutes

SMOKE TIME: 1½ to 2 hours

FOR THE CRUST

2 cups crushed gingersnap cookies (or Oreo or graham cracker crumbs)

6 tablespoons butter, melted, plus more for the pan

3 tablespoons firmly packed brown sugar

FOR THE FILLING

4 (8-ounce) packages cream cheese, at room temperature

4 eggs, beaten

1 cup sugar

1 teaspoon vanilla extract

FOR THE TOPPINGS (OPTIONAL)

Fresh berries

Whipped cream

Chocolate syrup

Caramel sauce

TO MAKE THE CRUST

1. In a food processor, pulse the cookie crumbs, butter, and brown sugar until combined.

2. Butter a springform pan and press the crumb mixture into the bottom and ½ inch up the sides.

TO MAKE THE FILLING

1. Preheat the smoker to 275°F with the apple, cherry, or peach wood.

2. In a large bowl, beat together the cream cheese, eggs, sugar, and vanilla until well blended. Pour the filling into the crust and place the pan inside the smoker. Fill a pan (any size that will fit on the rack next to the cheesecake) with 1 inch of water and place it in the smoker with the cheesecake. Smoke for 1½ to 2 hours until the cheesecake is firm.

3. Remove the cheesecake from the smoker, let it cool and then refrigerate it for 4 hours to set before serving with your toppings of choice.

VARIATION TIP: Cheesecake is truly one of those "blank canvas" desserts. Add 1 tablespoon lime zest and ½ cup Key lime juice, or ½ cup pumpkin purée, or ⅓ cup peanut butter, or an 11-ounce package of caramels (melted) to the filling for different flavor variations.

Cold-smoking can take a wimpy chunk of Cheddar and transform it into an epicurean treat that stands up to your finest wines and whiskies. The trick is to bathe the cheese in smoke while keeping the surroundings under 90°F. A few mainstream electric smokers do not have the ability to cold-smoke without an add-on, such as the Masterbuilt Cold Smoker, or an A-Maze-N brand slow-smoke box. Summertime heat and direct sun can also overheat cheese. Look for shade, wait for sundown, or reschedule for colder weather.

COLD-SMOKED CHEESES

MAKES 1 POUND | **SUB 90°F** | **APPLE**

MELLOWING TIME: 1 to 7 days
PREP TIME: 5 minutes
SMOKE TIME: 2 hours

1 pound Cheddar, Gouda, mozzarella, provolone, Swiss, or Pepper Jack cheese, cut into 4-by-2-inch blocks, at room temperature to avoid condensation and sweating in the smoker

1. Prepare the smoker for cold-smoking (under 90°F) with the applewood.

2. Blot the cheese completely dry with paper towels and place it in the coolest area of the smoker grate—typically away from the smoke source, near the wide-open ceiling vent. Allow steady smoke for 2 hours until the cheese displays a tint of smoke coloring.

3. Remove the cheese from the smoker and let it come to room temperature. Blot dry if necessary, wrap in parchment paper or wax paper, and refrigerate for 1 to 7 days for the smoke flavors to mellow.

SMOKING TIP: One technique to lower your smoke chamber's temperature is to add ice. Two-liter frozen water bottles can help.

Gouda is one of the most popular cheeses in the world. Named for the Dutch city from where it was first traded in the twelfth century, it is now more of a process than a kind of cheese and there are actually seven different categories of Gouda, based on age.

HOT-SMOKED GOUDA BACON DIP

SERVES 4 TO 6 | **CHEESE SUB 90°F, DIP 225°F** | **HICKORY OR MESQUITE**

MELLOWING TIME: 1 to 7 days

PREP TIME: 10 minutes

SMOKE TIME: cheese 2 hours, dip 1 hour

1 pound Gouda cheese, cut into 4-by-2-inch blocks, at room temperature

4 tablespoons butter

2 tablespoons all-purpose flour

1 cup whole milk

8 bacon slices, cooked and crumbled

Crackers or pita points, for serving

1. Prepare the smoker for cold-smoking (under 90°F) with the hickory or mesquite wood, and maintain the temperature.

2. Place the cheese blocks on the top rack and smoke for about 2 hours.

3. Remove the cheese from the smoker and wrap the smoked cheese blocks in parchment paper, wax paper, or vacuum pack them with a food sealer. Refrigerate for 1 to 7 days to mellow the flavor.

4. When ready to serve the dip, shred the smoked Gouda blocks (you should get about 1½ cups).

5. In a large saucepan over medium heat, melt the butter.

6. Whisk in the flour and continue whisking for 1 minute to make the roux.

7. Slowly add the milk and continue to whisk for about 5 minutes, or until thickened.

8. Stir in the smoked Gouda and bacon. Remove from the heat when the cheese melts.

9. Preheat the smoker to 225°F with the hickory or mesquite wood.

10. Transfer the dip into a small metal or aluminum-foil pan and place it in the smoker for 1 hour before serving to get that added smoke flavor and keep it hot.

11. Serve warm with crackers or pita points.

PREPARATION TIP: Of course, you can just buy smoked Gouda and make this dip, but it wouldn't be as impressive.

This is a great recipe for some of those beautiful, aromatic, Cold-Smoked Cheeses you smoked recently (page 153).

SMOKED TOMATO-MOZZARELLA DIP

SERVES 8 TO 10 | **275°F** | **MESQUITE**

PREP TIME: 5 minutes

SMOKE TIME: 1 hour

8 ounces smoked mozzarella cheese, shredded

8 ounces Colby cheese, shredded

½ cup grated Parmesan cheese

1 cup sour cream

1 cup sun-dried tomatoes

1½ teaspoons salt

1 teaspoon freshly ground black pepper

1 teaspoon dried basil

1 teaspoon dried oregano

1 teaspoon red pepper flakes

1 garlic clove, finely minced

½ teaspoon onion powder

Crackers or toasted French bread slices, for serving

1. Preheat the smoker to 275°F with the mesquite wood.

2. In a large bowl, stir together the mozzarella, Colby, Parmesan, sour cream, tomatoes, salt, pepper, basil, oregano, red pepper flakes, garlic, and onion powder. Transfer the mixture to a small metal or aluminum-foil pan. Place the pan in the smoker for 1 hour until hot and bubbly.

3. Serve hot with crackers or toasted French bread slices.

INGREDIENT TIP: Rather than using store-bought sun-dried tomatoes, smoke your own halved tomatoes seasoned with salt and pepper at 250°F, cut-side down, for 30 to 40 minutes.

Nothing beats a good party mix. If you don't like the ingredients suggested here, use 12 cups of any combination of your favorite small snack crackers, mini pretzels, nuts, raisins, cereals, etc. Salty, sweet, or spicy, it's always a favorite — but you better have plenty of beer on ice in the Yeti.

SPICY SMOKY SNACK MIX

MAKES 12 CUPS | **225°F** | **HICKORY OR MESQUITE**

PREP TIME: 10 minutes

SMOKE TIME: 2 to 2½ hours

Nonstick cooking spray

½ cup (1 stick) butter, melted

2 tablespoons Worcestershire sauce

1 teaspoon onion powder

1 teaspoon garlic powder

2 cups oyster crackers

2 cups mini pretzels

2 cups (16 ounces) honey-roasted peanuts

2 cups garlic bagel chips, broken

2 cups sesame sticks

2 cups Cheez-It crackers

1. Preheat the smoker to 225°F with the hickory or mesquite wood.

2. Line two rimmed baking sheets with parchment paper (or aluminum foil), and grease the parchment with nonstick cooking spray.

3. In a small bowl, stir together the butter, Worcestershire sauce, onion powder, and garlic powder.

4. In a large bowl, combine the oyster crackers, pretzels, peanuts, bagel chips, sesame sticks, and cheese crackers.

5. Pour the butter mixture over the snack mix and stir until all is well coated. Spread the snack mix in a single layer on the prepared baking sheets and place them inside the smoker. Smoke for 2 to 2½ hours until dry.

6. Store in an airtight container.

PREPARATION TIP: If you use traditional Chex cereals, add 1½ teaspoons of salt to the recipe. Make it in bulk during the holidays and deliver to friends in a cute tub or tin. I've been told a repurposed Country Crock tub is not cute.

Almonds have been proclaimed a superfood for all their healthy nutritional attributes. Unfortunately, my doctor only wants me to eat them raw. I meet him halfway. Buy them raw and gently smoke 'em low and slow. I promise to try to stop at just a handful.

SMOKEHOUSE ALMONDS

MAKES 2 CUPS | **225°F** | **HICKORY OR MESQUITE**

MELLOWING TIME: Overnight
PREP TIME: 10 minutes
SMOKE TIME: 1 hour

Nonstick cooking spray
3 tablespoons butter, melted
2½ teaspoons garlic powder
2 teaspoons salt
1 teaspoon freshly ground black pepper
1 teaspoon onion powder
1 teaspoon dried thyme
2 cups (16 ounces) raw almonds

1. Preheat the smoker to 225°F with the hickory or mesquite wood.

2. Line a rimmed baking sheet with parchment paper (or aluminum foil), and grease the parchment with nonstick cooking spray.

3. In a medium bowl, stir together the butter, garlic powder, salt, pepper, onion powder, and thyme.

4. Add the almonds and stir until they are well coated. Arrange the nuts in a single layer on the prepared baking sheet. Place the sheet in the smoker and smoke for about 1 hour, turning once.

5. Remove from the smoker and let the nuts cool. Dry overnight and store in an airtight container away from heat, light, and moisture.

SMOKING TIP: As with smoked cheese, a "rest" helps enhance the smoked flavor of nuts.

Okay nut nerds, I confess...the almond is not scientifically a nut. It's actually a drupe, which is a kind of stone fruit. They are also members of the rose family and contain the most calcium of any of the snack "nuts." And cashews? They grow from the bottoms of cashew apples. The cashew apples alone aren't all that tasty, but the crescent-shaped morsels we know and love are the perfect companions to almonds in this savory mix. You won't be able to stop at just a handful.

BARBECUE ALMONDS AND CASHEWS

MAKES 2 CUPS | **225°F** | **HICKORY OR PECAN**

MELLOWING TIME: Overnight
PREP TIME: 10 minutes
SMOKE TIME: 1 hour

Nonstick cooking spray
1 large egg white
1 tablespoon water
1 cup (8 ounces) raw almonds
1 cup (8 ounces) raw cashews
½ cup Bill's Best Barbecue Rub (page 170)

1. Preheat the smoker to 225°F with the hickory or pecan wood.

2. Line a rimmed baking sheet with parchment paper (or aluminum foil), and grease the parchment with nonstick cooking spray.

3. In a medium bowl, whisk the egg white and water.

4. Stir in the almonds and cashews until they are well coated. Arrange the nuts in a single layer on the prepared baking sheet.

5. Sprinkle with the rub.

6. Place the sheet in the smoker and smoke for about 1 hour, turning once.

7. Remove from the smoker and let the nuts cool. Dry overnight to enhance the smoke flavor.

8. Break up any clusters and store the nuts in an airtight container.

INGREDIENT TIP: Nuts are widely available already roasted, but you need raw nuts for this recipe. Whole Foods and Trader Joe's sell a lot of nuts and are a good choice for the freshest selection.

Make it easy for the smoke to adhere to the nuts by starting with a wet coating and grill pan (or tray with plenty of holes). Frogmats are heat-resistant, nonstick mesh mats that are perfect for letting smoke flow around your food. They're also machine washable. But, when you start smoking with sugars, as in this recipe, things tend to get so sticky that I recommend using greased parchment paper on a grill pan.

GLAZED SPICED PECANS

MAKES 2 CUPS | **225°F** | **APPLE, PEACH, OR PEAR**

MELLOWING TIME: Overnight
PREP TIME: 10 minutes
SMOKE TIME: 1 hour

Nonstick cooking spray
¼ cup firmly packed brown sugar
1 tablespoon butter, melted
1 tablespoon light corn syrup
1 teaspoon ground cinnamon
2 teaspoons salt
2 cups (16 ounces) pecan halves

1. Preheat the smoker to 225°F with the apple, peach, or pear wood.

2. Line a rimmed baking sheet with parchment paper (or aluminum foil), and grease the parchment with nonstick cooking spray.

3. In a medium bowl, stir together the brown sugar, butter, corn syrup, cinnamon, and salt.

4. Add the nuts and stir until they are well coated. Arrange the nuts in a single layer on the prepared baking sheet. Place the sheet in the smoker and smoke for about 1 hour, turning once. Look for a glazed finish and roasted aroma.

5. When done, remove the nuts from the smoker and let them cool. Dry them overnight to enhance the flavor.

6. Store in an airtight container.

PREPARATION TIP: Add even more spice to your pecans with cayenne, cumin, chili powder, nutmeg, or cocoa powder.

Spicy Hickory-Smoked Barbecue Sauce, page 163

163 Spicy Hickory-Smoked Barbecue Sauce

164 Carolina Mustard Sauce

165 Hot Pepper Vinegar Barbecue Sauce

166 Bleu Cheese Cowboy Butter

167 Alabama White Sauce

168 Pineapple–Brown Sugar Sauce

169 Chimichurri Sauce

170 Bill's Best Barbecue Rub

171 Java Rub

172 Plum Sauce

173 Smoky Teriyaki Marinade

TEN

SAUCES, RUBS & MORE

When smoking meat or vegetables, the sauce is secondary to the smoke. Some really proud pit masters scoff at saucing the meat and ask that it only be served on the side. I recommend a rub before smoking and saucing at the end, either as a glaze or on the side. Mark your map: Some regional-favorite sauces include South Carolina's mustard-based sauces, North Carolina's vinegar-based sauces, Alabama's unusual white sauce for chicken and, of course, Kansas City's sweet smoky sauce that is on store shelves nationwide as KC Masterpiece.

Lately, the trend in sauces is offering a large variety, with one major sauce maker releasing a five-bottle sampler of regional sauces. Variety is the spice—and sauce—of life!

TIPS FOR BARBECUE SAUCE SUCCESS

Keep things saucy (and sassy) by following these tips:

- Never reuse or serve sauces or marinades that have made contact with uncooked meat. It is the most common way for dangerous bacteria to be transferred, and could potentially cause food poisoning.

- Add hot sauces to hot food and cold sauces to cold food.

- When cooking, add sweet sauces at the end of the cooking process. This prevents temperature-sensitive sugar from burning.

- Use nonreactive containers to prepare your sauces. Good choices are stainless steel, glass, enamel, and porcelain vessels that will not cause a chemical reaction when in contact with acidic foods.

- Burn off alcohol before using in marinades. Food expert Harold McGee says alcohol dehydrates red meat and fish tissues.

My wife says she could drink this sauce. Of course you can simmer it on the stovetop, but it really adds extra hickory flavor to smoke it. This is excellent basted on chicken.

SPICY HICKORY-SMOKED BARBECUE SAUCE

MAKES 3 CUPS | **225°F** | **HICKORY**

PREP TIME: 30 minutes

SMOKE TIME: 30 minutes

1 small onion, finely chopped

2 garlic cloves, finely minced

2 cups ketchup

1 cup water

½ cup molasses

½ cup apple cider vinegar

5 tablespoons granulated sugar

5 tablespoons firmly packed brown sugar

1 tablespoon Worcestershire sauce

1 tablespoon freshly squeezed lemon juice

2 teaspoons hickory liquid smoke

1½ teaspoons freshly ground black pepper

1½ teaspoons dry mustard

1. Preheat the smoker to 225°F with the hickory wood.

2. In a saucepan over medium heat, stir together the onion, garlic, ketchup, water, molasses, vinegar, granulated sugar, brown sugar, Worcestershire sauce, lemon juice, liquid smoke, pepper, and mustard. Bring to a boil. Transfer the sauce to a small metal or aluminum-foil pan and place it in the smoker for 30 minutes to absorb the smoke's flavor.

3. If you prefer a smooth sauce, strain out the chunks before serving. Refrigerate in an airtight container for up to 2 weeks.

PREPARATION TIP: Add 1 chopped bell pepper and 1 cup leftover pulled pork to this recipe and don't strain it after cooking. Serve over cooked angel-hair pasta for barbecue spaghetti.

This is often called Carolina Gold around South Carolina where the Bessinger family has built a mustard empire with their secret-recipe mustard sauce. Some say the mustard infusion came from the many German immigrants in South Carolina over the years. This makes a sweet-and-tangy sauce that's great served with barbecue.

CAROLINA MUSTARD SAUCE

MAKES 1 CUP

PREP TIME: 10 minutes

¾ cup prepared yellow mustard

¼ cup maple syrup

¼ cup apple cider vinegar

2 tablespoons firmly packed brown sugar

2 tablespoons ketchup

1 tablespoon Worcestershire sauce

2 teaspoons hot sauce

1 teaspoon pumpkin-pie spice

1 teaspoon salt

1 teaspoon freshly ground black pepper

In a medium bowl, whisk the mustard, maple syrup, vinegar, brown sugar, ketchup, Worcestershire sauce, hot sauce, pumpkin-pie spice, salt, and pepper. Refrigerate in an airtight container for up to 2 weeks.

PAIR IT: Mustard pairs well with pork. Use this flavorful sauce with the Hickory-Smoked Pork Loin (page 65).

VARIATION TIP: Toast ¼ cup chopped pecans, stir them into the sauce, and pour over a block of cream cheese. Serve with crackers. Yum!

Hot pepper vinegar is from a bottle of pickled peppers in a vinegar brine with hot spices. It provides the heat and the sour in this sweet-and-spicy sauce. This is an excellent sauce for pulled pork or brisket.

HOT PEPPER VINEGAR BARBECUE SAUCE

MAKES 3 CUPS

PREP TIME: 30 minutes

2 cups ketchup

1 cup firmly packed light-brown sugar

1 cup hot-pepper vinegar sauce

2 tablespoons white vinegar

2 tablespoons salt

1 tablespoon chili powder

2 teaspoons freshly ground black pepper

1 teaspoon garlic powder

1 teaspoon cayenne pepper

½ teaspoon ground allspice

In a saucepan over medium heat, stir together the ketchup, brown sugar, hot-pepper vinegar sauce, white vinegar, salt, chili powder, pepper, garlic powder, cayenne, and allspice. Bring to a boil, reduce the heat to low, and simmer, covered, for 25 minutes, stirring occasionally. Refrigerate in an airtight container for up to 2 weeks.

PAIR IT: Give Peppercorn Pork Tenderloin (page 57) an even spicier edge.

If you haven't experimented with flavored herb butters, here is an easy one to dress up your next cookout.

BLEU CHEESE COWBOY BUTTER

MAKES 1 CUP

PREP TIME: 5 minutes

1 cup unsalted butter, softened

4 ounce bleu cheese crumbles, room temperature

1 teaspoon cayenne pepper

1 teaspoon garlic powder

¼ cup chopped scallions, white and green parts

1 tablespoon brown sugar, firmly packed

1. Cream the butter and bleu cheese with a mixer.

2. Add the cayenne pepper, garlic powder, scallions, and brown sugar, and blend well.

3. Using wax paper, roll the mixture into a cylindrical log and wrap well.

4. Refrigerate for a minimum of 4 hours.

5. When ready to serve, unwrap and cut into 1-inch slices.

SERVING TIP: Serve a slice on Smoked Prime Rib (page 83) for a burst of flavor.

VARIATION TIP: Add 4 slices of cooked, crumbled bacon and ½ cup of finely chopped Glazed Spiced Pecans (page 159) for a different flavor combination.

In Alabama, this mayonnaise-based sauce is preferred over the ketchup-, mustard-, and vinegar-based sauces of the rest of the South. Although this is called a barbecue sauce, it isn't really for pork. Chicken is the way to go here. It can also be used as a quick coleslaw dressing.

ALABAMA WHITE SAUCE

MAKES 1 CUP

PREP TIME: 10 minutes

1 cup mayonnaise

¼ cup apple cider vinegar

1 tablespoon hot chili powder

1 teaspoon
Worcestershire sauce

½ teaspoon celery seed

½ teaspoon red pepper flakes

¼ teaspoon cayenne pepper

Salt

Freshly ground black pepper

1. In a medium bowl, whisk the mayonnaise, vinegar, chili powder, Worcestershire sauce, celery seed, red pepper flakes, and cayenne until well blended. Season with salt and pepper and whisk again to combine.

2. Refrigerate in an airtight container for up to 2 weeks.

PAIR IT: Serve with Smoked Beer-Can Chicken (page 36) for an unexpected treat.

This sauce is a hopped-up traditional ham glaze, but if you like it sweet it's good with barbecue, too. This sweet-and-sour sauce is excellent with ham and brisket.

PINEAPPLE-BROWN SUGAR SAUCE

MAKES 2 CUPS

PREP TIME: 10 minutes

1 (20-ounce) can pineapple chunks, with juice

1 cup firmly packed brown sugar

2 tablespoons prepared mustard

2 tablespoons tomato paste

1 tablespoon ground cloves

1 teaspoon ground nutmeg

1 teaspoon ground cinnamon

1 teaspoon ancho chile powder (or chipotle)

In a large bowl, combine the pineapple chunks and juice, brown sugar, mustard, tomato paste, cloves, nutmeg, cinnamon, and chile powder. Stir well to mix. Refrigerate in an airtight container for up to 2 weeks.

PAIR IT: Sweeten your Holiday Ham (page 71) or Smoked Cauliflower Steaks (page 145).

Chimichurri sauce is a garlic- and parsley-based sauce origin-ally from Argentina. I love it on steak, but it is fresh and delicious on just about any smoked meat. Try it with beef, chicken, and lamb.

CHIMICHURRI SAUCE

MAKES 1 CUP

PREP TIME: 10 minutes

½ cup olive oil

2 tablespoons fresh oregano leaves

2 tablespoons chopped fresh parsley leaves

2 tablespoons minced garlic

2 tablespoons red wine vinegar

2 teaspoons red pepper flakes

Salt

Freshly ground black pepper

In a food processor or blender, combine the olive oil, oregano, parsley, garlic, vinegar, and red pepper flakes. Season with salt and pepper and pulse until smooth. Refrigerate in an airtight container for up to 2 weeks.

PAIR IT: Chimichurri will brighten the flavors of Smoked Prime Rib (page 83), Herb-Smoked Quail (page 37), or Rack of Lamb (page 123).

I created this delicious, but spicy, rub years ago for smoking a whole hog, but now I always keep it on hand to use as a general spice rub. It is perfect for pork and chicken. Use it with olive oil on the meat and marinate it for an hour in the refrigerator, or simply sprinkle it on right before the meat goes into the smoker. Omit the cayenne pepper if you need to cut the heat.

BILL'S BEST BARBECUE RUB

MAKES ¾ CUP

PREP TIME: 10 minutes

¼ cup paprika

¼ cup Sugar In The Raw, or other turbinado sugar

3 tablespoons Cajun seasoning

1 tablespoon firmly packed brown sugar

1½ teaspoons chili powder

1½ teaspoons cayenne pepper

1½ teaspoons ground cumin

In a small bowl, stir together the paprika, sugar, Cajun seasoning, brown sugar, chili powder, cayenne, and cumin. Refrigerate in an airtight container for up to 2 weeks.

PAIR IT: To mix it up, try this rub on okra or green beans drizzled with olive oil and roasted in a 400°F oven for 30 minutes.

Coffee is native to tropical Africa and Madagascar. Known as a stimulant since its discovery in the 1500s, coffee beans are now grown in more than 70 countries, and coffee is now one of the most popular drinks in the world. This recipe produces a flavorful dry rub.

JAVA RUB

MAKES 1 CUP

PREP TIME: 10 minutes

¼ cup finely ground roasted coffee beans

¼ cup paprika

¼ cup garlic powder

2 tablespoons chili powder

1 tablespoon firmly packed light-brown sugar

1 tablespoon ground allspice

1 tablespoon ground coriander

1 tablespoon freshly ground black pepper

2 teaspoons dry mustard

1½ teaspoons celery seed

In a blender or food processor, combine the coffee beans, paprika, garlic powder, chili powder, brown sugar, allspice, coriander, pepper, mustard, and celery seed. Pulse until fine. Store in an airtight container for up to 3 months, after which it starts to lose its flavor.

PAIR IT: This will add a new dimension to your Juicy Beef Short Ribs (page 80), or try it on chicken thighs.

Plums are easy to find because they grow during different times of the year all over the globe. They have many uses, such as in jams, wines, and even dried as prunes. I created this sauce specifically for my Plum Chicken Pops (page 50), but it is good as a dipping sauce for meat and veggies, too.

PLUM SAUCE

MAKES 1 CUP

PREP TIME: 30 minutes

12 ounces plum jam

2 tablespoons apple cider vinegar

1 tablespoon firmly packed brown sugar

1 tablespoon dry minced onion

1 teaspoon red pepper flakes

1 garlic clove, minced

½ teaspoon ground ginger

Salt

Freshly ground black pepper

1. In a medium saucepan over high heat, whisk together the jam, vinegar, brown sugar, onion, red pepper flakes, garlic, and ginger. Season with salt and pepper and bring to a boil.

2. Reduce the heat to low and simmer for about 20 minutes.

3. Refrigerate in an airtight container for up to 2 weeks.

PAIR IT: Serve with Plum Chicken Pops (page 50), or serve as a dipping sauce for Chipotle Wings (page 41) or Smoked Bacon-Wrapped Onion Rings (page 138).

When my wife and I first used this recipe, we spilled a little marinade on the deck. That night all the neighborhood cats showed up. We figured they had good taste! The smoky sweet flavor is excellent for steak and chicken.

SMOKY TERIYAKI MARINADE

MAKES 1½ CUPS

PREP TIME: 10 minutes

½ cup low-sodium soy sauce

½ cup teriyaki sauce

¼ cup firmly packed brown sugar

¼ cup granulated sugar

1 small onion, finely chopped

¼ cup rice wine vinegar

¼ cup canola oil

3 tablespoons hoisin sauce

2 teaspoons ground ginger

1 tablespoon minced garlic

1 teaspoon liquid smoke

1. In a small bowl, stir together the soy sauce, teriyaki sauce, brown sugar, and granulated sugar until dissolved and well blended.

2. Add the onion, vinegar, oil, hoisin sauce, ginger, garlic, and liquid smoke. Stir to combine.

3. Pour it over your steak as a marinade, or bring to a boil and serve as a sauce for steak or chicken. Refrigerate any leftovers in an airtight container for up to 2 weeks (but this is so good you won't have any left!).

PAIR IT: Try this with T-Bone Kebabs (page 81).

MEASUREMENT CONVERSIONS

VOLUME EQUIVALENTS (LIQUID)

US STANDARD	US STANDARD (OUNCES)	METRIC (APPROXIMATE)
2 tablespoons	1 fl. oz.	30 mL
¼ cup	2 fl. oz.	60 mL
½ cup	4 fl. oz.	120 mL
1 cup	8 fl. oz.	240 mL
1 ½ cups	12 fl. oz.	355 mL
2 cups or 1 pint	16 fl. oz.	475 mL
4 cups or 1 quart	32 fl. oz.	1 L
1 gallon	128 fl. oz.	4 L

OVEN TEMPERATURES

FAHRENHEIT	CELSIUS (APPROXIMATE)
250°F	120°C
300°F	150°C
325°F	165°C
350°F	180°C
375°F	190°C
400°F	200°C
425°F	220°C
450°F	230°C

VOLUME EQUIVALENTS (DRY)

US STANDARD	METRIC (APPROXIMATE)
⅛ teaspoon	0.5 mL
¼ teaspoon	1 mL
½ teaspoon	2 mL
¾ teaspoon	4 mL
1 teaspoon	5 mL
1 tablespoon	15 mL
¼ cup	59 mL
⅓ cup	79 mL
½ cup	118 mL
⅔ cup	156 mL
¾ cup	177 mL
1 cup	235 mL
2 cups or 1 pint	475 mL
3 cups	700 mL
4 cups or 1 quart	1 L

WEIGHT EQUIVALENTS

US STANDARD	METRIC (APPROXIMATE)
½ ounce	15 g
1 ounce	30 g
2 ounces	60 g
4 ounces	115 g
8 ounces	225 g
12 ounces	340 g
16 ounces or 1 pound	455 g

RESOURCES

WEB SITES

Barbecue Tricks:

BarbecueTricks.com/resources

Much of the woodchip selection and cooking-temperature guides in this book were first tested at my site that I founded earlier this century. You can find my personal barbecue resources here.

Bradley Smoker:

North-America.BradleySmoker.com/food -smokers/original-electric-food-smoker

Head to each electric smoker model's product page for details and downloadable owner manuals.

Carolina Pit Masters:

CarolinaPitMasters.com

Jack Waiboer offers the quintessential class on barbecuing from patio to competition pit master.

Char-Broil:

CharBroil.com/deluxe-digital-electric-smoker

Head to each electric smoker model's product page for details and downloadable owner manuals.

Cooking Everything Outdoors:

Cooking-Outdoors.com/cleaning-and -maintaining-a-food-smoker

Gary House is a prolific barbecue blogger and this is a go-to site for any recipe that might involve smoke.

GrateTV:

GrateTV.com

Many of the slow-smoke techniques discussed in this book were originally revealed in various episodes of my online video series. Along with friend Jack Waiboer, we shared weekly adventures in live-fire cooking and barbecue.

Honest-Food.net:

Honest-Food.net

Hunter-angler-gardener-cook Hank Shaw, with his camouflage apron, is the writer and podcaster behind this James Beard Award–winning food blog.

Jack Daniel's:

JackDaniels.com

Even a visit to their distillery in Lynchburg couldn't give me all the details about how fire and charcoal combine to make this Tennessee whiskey.

Liquor and Wine Outlets Blog:

LiquorAndWineOutlets.com/blog/2014/11

The New Hampshire liquor and wine seller has a lot of recipe and food-pairing information worth a long read in the blog.

Masterbuilt:

Masterbuilt.com

Head to each electric smoker model's product page for details and downloadable owner manuals.

Serious Eats:

SeriousEats.com/2015/08/how-to-pick -shrimp-varieties-freshness-guide.html

The Serious Eats website is the world's most trusted authority on deliciousness. Their guides to shrimp are especially informative.

Snake River Farms:

SnakeRiverFarms.com/preparation-guides

Snake River Farms is one of the few sources of Wagyu brisket. The website also offers detailed cooking guides with specialty beef and pork information.

Virtual Weber Bullet:

VirtualWeberBullet.com/storing.html

The Virtual Weber Bullet site offers a vast library of knowledge that is primarily focused on Weber's popular charcoal Smokey Mountain Cooker but also features an active community of smokers.

BOOKS

Goldwyn, Meathead. *Meathead: The Science of Great Barbecue and Grilling.* New York: Rux Martin/Houghton Mifflin Harcourt, 2016.

Meathead is the founder of the Amazing Ribs website and has distilled the site into this manual of meat. Lots of smoker science is revealed.

Raichlen, Steven. *Project Smoke: Seven Steps to Smoked Food Nirvana.* New York: Workman Publishing, 2016.

There is now a third season of Raichlen's show based on this book. Lots of Bradley Smoker testing in the show and in the book.

West, Bill. *BBQ Blueprint: Top Tricks, Recipes, and Secret Ingredients to Help Make You Champion of the Grill,* 2016.

Many of the recipes and techniques noted in this book were foreshadowed in my first book, available from Amazon.com, plus downloadable pit-master and cooking logs.

RECIPE INDEX

A

Alabama White Sauce, 167
Applewood-Smoked Turkey Breast, 45
Armadillo "Eggs," 126

B

Baba Ghanouj, 124
Bacon-Wrapped Crab-Stuffed Shrimp, 108
Barbecue Almonds and Cashews, 158
Big Fat Greek Fatty, 127
Big McFatty, 90
Bill's Best Barbecue Rub, 170
Bleu Cheese Cowboy Butter, 166
Bourbon-Marinated Beef Roast, 85
Breakfast Fatty, 119
Buffalo Chicken Balls, 39

C

Cajun Alligator Appetizer, 115
Cajun Shrimp, 107
Caramelized Honey Buffalo Chicken, 49
Carolina Mustard Sauce, 164
Carolina Pulled Pork Bites, 68
Chimichurri Sauce, 169
Chipotle Wings, 41
Cinnamon-Cured Fire-Smoked Chicken, 47
Citrus and Garlic Scallops, 106
Cold-Smoked Cheeses, 153
Competition Baby Back Ribs, 58
Country Cajun Catfish, 100
Crab-Stuffed Tomato, 109
Crispy-Skin Orange Chicken, 38
Cuban Mojo-Marinated Pork, 66

D

Drunken Drumsticks, 42–43

F

Fireball Whiskey Meatballs, 77–78

G

Garlic-Herb Turkey Legs, 40
Garlic-Rosemary Potato Wedges, 136
Glazed Spiced Pecans, 159

H

Hasselback Sweet Potatoes, 140
Herb-Smoked Quail, 37
Hickory-Smoked Pork Loin, 65
Holiday Ham, 71
Homemade Bacon, 61
Hot Pepper Vinegar Barbecue Sauce, 165
Hot-Smoked Gouda Bacon Dip, 154

J

Jamaican Jerk Chicken, 46
Java Rub, 171
Juicy Beef Short Ribs, 80

L

Lemon Pepper Bacon-Wrapped Trout, 95
Loaded Hasselback Potatoes, 135

M

Maple-Glazed Salmon, 96
Mesquite Maple-Bacon Chicken, 51

P

Peppercorn Pork Tenderloin, 57
Peppercorn Tuna Steaks, 98
Pig Candy, 62
Pineapple–Brown Sugar Sauce, 168
Pineapple Pigtail, 116
Plum Chicken Pops, 50
Plum Sauce, 172
Porchetta Italian Pork Belly Roast, 118

Pork Italian Sausage Fatty, 56
Potato Bacon Bites, 143

R

Rack of Lamb, 123

S

Scuppernong Lobster, 103
Simple Smoked Pork Shoulder, 67
Slow-Smoked Ancho Chile-Rubbed
    Boston Butt, 59–60
Smoked Artichokes, 139
Smoked Asparagus, 137
Smoked Bacon-Wrapped Onion Rings, 138
Smoked Beef Brisket Chili, 87
Smoked Beef Jerky, 84
Smoked Beer Can Chicken, 36
Smoked Bologna, 125
Smoked Brie with Brown Sugar and Pecans, 151
Smoked Brisket and Cheese Pizza, 91
Smoked Brisket Grilled Cheese, 89
Smoked Cabbage, 134
Smoked Cauliflower Steaks, 145
Smoked Cheesecake, 152
Smoked Chorizo-Stuffed Peppers, 122
Smoked Chuck Roast, 86
Smoked Coleslaw, 131
Smoked Corn on the Cob, 142
Smoked Deviled Eggs, 141
Smoked Halibut, 99
Smoked Italian Sausage, 69
Smoked Jalapeño Cheese-Stuffed Pork Balls, 64
Smoked Lobster Tails, 102
Smoked Mac and Cheese, 149

Smoked Meat Loaf, 82
Smoked Onion Bombs, 133
Smoked Peach Parfait, 121
Smoked Pork Pinwheels, 70
Smoked Prime Rib, 83
Smoked Sausage Hash, 63
Smoked Seasoned Duck, 113
Smoked Shrimp and Scallops, 105
Smoked Spaghetti Squash, 144
Smoked Stuffed Pumpkin Squash, 117
Smoked Tomato-Mozzarella Dip, 155
Smoked Tri-Tip Roast, 76
Smoked Venison Steaks, 114
Smokehouse Almonds, 157
Smoky Brined Turkey, 48
Smoky Oysters, 104
Smoky Teriyaki Marinade, 173
Spicy Hickory-Smoked Barbecue Sauce, 163
Spicy Korean Rib Eye Barbecue, 88
Spicy Piggy Mac, 150
Spicy Smoky Snack Mix, 156
Stuffed Cornish Game Hens, 120
Stuffed Jalapeños, 132
Succulent Salmon Nuggets, 97
Sugared Sea Bass, 101
Sweet Sriracha Barbecue Chicken, 44

T

T-Bone Kebabs, 81

U

Unbelievably Moist Brisket, 79

INDEX

A

Almonds
Barbecue Almonds and Cashews, 158
Smokehouse Almonds, 157
American cheese
Big McFatty, 90
Smoked Brisket and Cheese Pizza, 91
Apples
Smoked Brie with Brown Sugar and Pecans, 151
Smoky Brined Turkey, 48
Artichokes
Smoked Artichokes, 139
Asparagus
Smoked Asparagus, 137
Avocados
Cuban Mojo-Marinated Pork, 66
Smoked Brisket Grilled Cheese, 89

B

Bacon
Bacon-Wrapped Crab-Stuffed Shrimp, 108
Big McFatty, 90
Breakfast Fatty, 119
Carolina Pulled Pork Bites, 68
Fireball Whiskey Meatballs, 77–78
Homemade Bacon, 61
Hot-Smoked Gouda Bacon Dip, 154
Lemon Pepper Bacon-Wrapped Trout, 95
Loaded Hasselback Potatoes, 135
Mesquite Maple-Bacon Chicken, 51
Pig Candy, 62
Pineapple Pigtail, 116
Pork Italian Sausage Fatty, 56
Potato Bacon Bites, 143
Smoked Bacon-Wrapped Onion Rings, 138
Smoked Chorizo-Stuffed Peppers, 122
Smoked Jalapeño Cheese-Stuffed Pork Balls, 64
Spicy Piggy Mac, 150
Stuffed Jalapeños, 132
Banana peppers
Pork Italian Sausage Fatty, 56
Bear "claws," 9
Beef
Big Fat Greek Fatty, 127
Big McFatty, 90
Bourbon-Marinated Beef Roast, 85
cuts, 15, 74
Fireball Whiskey Meatballs, 77–78
grades, 74
Juicy Beef Short Ribs, 80
Smoked Beef Brisket Chili, 87
Smoked Beef Jerky, 84
Smoked Brisket and Cheese Pizza, 91
Smoked Brisket Grilled Cheese, 89
Smoked Chuck Roast, 86
Smoked Meat Loaf, 82
Smoked Prime Rib, 83
Smoked Tri-Tip Roast, 76
smoking chart, 14
Spicy Korean Rib Eye Barbecue, 88
T-Bone Kebabs, 81
techniques, 73–75
Unbelievably Moist Brisket, 79
Beer
Drunken Drumsticks, 42–43
pairing with smoked foods, 28–29
Smoked Beef Brisket Chili, 87
Smoked Beer Can Chicken, 36
Bell peppers
Breakfast Fatty, 119
Pork Italian Sausage Fatty, 56
Smoked Brisket and Cheese Pizza, 91
Smoked Sausage Hash, 63
T-Bone Kebabs, 81

Beverages, 28–29

Bisquette savers, 9

Bleu cheese
    Bleu Cheese Cowboy Butter, 166
    Buffalo Chicken Balls, 39

Bourbon
    Bourbon-Marinated Beef Roast, 85

Bradley smokers, 5–6

Brie
    Smoked Brie with Brown Sugar and Pecans, 151

Brining, 34

Brooks, Kix, 73

Buttermilk
    Sugared Sea Bass, 101

C

Cabbage
    Smoked Cabbage, 134
    Smoked Coleslaw, 131

Capers
    Smoked Asparagus, 137

Carrots
    Smoked Coleslaw, 131

Cashews
    Barbecue Almonds and Cashews, 158

Cast iron skillets, 9

Cauliflower
    Smoked Cauliflower Steaks, 145

Celery
    Smoked Jalapeño Cheese-Stuffed Pork Balls, 64
    Smoked Stuffed Pumpkin Squash, 117

Char-Broil smokers, 5–6

Cheddar cheese
    Armadillo "Eggs," 126
    Breakfast Fatty, 119
    Buffalo Chicken Balls, 39
    Loaded Hasselback Potatoes, 135
    Potato Bacon Bites, 143
    Smoked Brisket Grilled Cheese, 89
    Smoked Chorizo-Stuffed Peppers, 122
    Smoked Jalapeño Cheese-Stuffed Pork Balls, 64
    Smoked Mac and Cheese, 149

    Spicy Piggy Mac, 150
    Stuffed Jalapeños, 132

Cheese. *See also specific*
    Cold-Smoked Cheeses, 153
    smoking, 148

Cherry peppers
    Loaded Hasselback Potatoes, 135

Chicken
    Buffalo Chicken Balls, 39
    Caramelized Honey Buffalo Chicken, 49
    Chipotle Wings, 41
    Cinnamon-Cured Fire-Smoked Chicken, 47
    Crispy-Skin Orange Chicken, 38
    cuts, 34
    Drunken Drumsticks, 42–43
    Jamaican Jerk Chicken, 46
    Mesquite Maple-Bacon Chicken, 51
    Plum Chicken Pops, 50
    Smoked Beer Can Chicken, 36
    smoking chart, 16
    Sweet Sriracha Barbecue Chicken, 44
    techniques, 34–35

Chili powder, 87

Chipotle peppers
    Chipotle Wings, 41
    Smoked Corn on the Cob, 142

Chives
    Drunken Drumsticks, 42–43
    Smoked Pork Pinwheels, 70

Cilantro
    Smoked Corn on the Cob, 142

Colby cheese
    Smoked Tomato-Mozzarella Dip, 155

Cold-smoking, 7–8, 148

Columbus, Christopher, 53

Cookouts, 26–28

Corn
    Smoked Corn on the Cob, 142

Crabmeat
    Bacon-Wrapped Crab-Stuffed Shrimp, 108
    Crab-Stuffed Tomato, 109

Cream
    Smoked Coleslaw, 131
    Spicy Piggy Mac, 150
Cream cheese
    Armadillo "Eggs," 126
    Maple-Glazed Salmon, 96
    Smoked Cheesecake, 152
    Smoked Mac and Cheese, 149
    Smoked Pork Pinwheels, 70
    Spicy Piggy Mac, 150
    Stuffed Jalapeños, 132
Cucumbers
    Big Fat Greek Fatty, 127
Curing, 3–4

D
Dehydrating, 8
Dill
    Big Fat Greek Fatty, 127
Dry brining, 34

E
Eggplant
    Baba Ghanouj, 124
Eggs
    Breakfast Fatty, 119
    Smoked Cheesecake, 152
    Smoked Deviled Eggs, 141
Electric knives, 9
Electric smokers. *See also* Smoking
    benefits of, 4
    brands, 4–6
    foods for, 16–18
    maintenance tips, 11
    optional gear, 8–9
    safety basics, 10–11
    temperatures, 7–8

F
Fish. *See also* Salmon
    Country Cajun Catfish, 100
    cuts, 94
    Lemon Pepper Bacon-Wrapped Trout, 95

Peppercorn Tuna Steaks, 98
    Smoked Halibut, 99
    smoking chart, 16
    Sugared Sea Bass, 101
    techniques, 93–94
Food preservation, 3–4, 25–26
Food safety, 8, 18, 54
Food storage, 25–26
Freezing foods, 25–26
Frogmats, 9
Fruits. *See also specific*
    smoking chart, 16–17

G
Garlic
    Baba Ghanouj, 124
    Big Fat Greek Fatty, 127
    Chimichurri Sauce, 169
    Citrus and Garlic Scallops, 106
    Cuban Mojo-Marinated Pork, 66
    Drunken Drumsticks, 42–43
    Fireball Whiskey Meatballs, 77–78
    Garlic-Herb Turkey Legs, 40
    Garlic-Rosemary Potato Wedges, 136
    Smoked Artichokes, 139
    Smoked Asparagus, 137
    Smoked Beef Brisket Chili, 87
    Smoked Brisket and Cheese Pizza, 91
    Smoked Cabbage, 134
    Smoked Cauliflower Steaks, 145
    Smoked Lobster Tails, 102
    Smoked Meat Loaf, 82
    Smoked Sausage Hash, 63
    Smoked Shrimp and Scallops, 105
    Smoked Tomato-Mozzarella Dip, 155
    Smoky Oysters, 104
    Smoky Teriyaki Marinade, 173
    Spicy Hickory-Smoked Barbecue Sauce, 163
    Spicy Korean Rib Eye Barbecue, 88
    Succulent Salmon Nuggets, 97
Giardiniera peppers
    Pork Italian Sausage Fatty, 56

Goat cheese
    Smoked Brisket Grilled Cheese, 89
Gouda cheese
    Carolina Pulled Pork Bites, 68
    Hot-Smoked Gouda Bacon Dip, 154
Grapes
    Scuppernong Lobster, 103
Gruyère cheese
    Smoked Brisket Grilled Cheese, 89

H

Habanero peppers
    Jamaican Jerk Chicken, 46
Hardwood planks, 9
Herbs, 23. *See also specific*
Honey
    Caramelized Honey Buffalo Chicken, 49
    Cuban Mojo-Marinated Pork, 66
    Hasselback Sweet Potatoes, 140
    Smoked Beef Jerky, 84
    Smoked Peach Parfait, 121
    Smoked Seasoned Duck, 113
    Spicy Korean Rib Eye Barbecue, 88

I

Injecting, 34

J

Jalapeño peppers
    Armadillo "Eggs," 126
    Chipotle Wings, 41
    Loaded Hasselback Potatoes, 135
    Smoked Jalapeño Cheese-Stuffed Pork Balls, 64
    Spicy Piggy Mac, 150
    Stuffed Jalapeños, 132

K

Kidney beans
    Smoked Beef Brisket Chili, 87

L

Lemons and lemon juice
    Baba Ghanouj, 124

Bacon-Wrapped Crab-Stuffed Shrimp, 108
Big Fat Greek Fatty, 127
Bourbon-Marinated Beef Roast, 85
Cinnamon-Cured Fire-Smoked Chicken, 47
Citrus and Garlic Scallops, 106
Crab-Stuffed Tomato, 109
Lemon Pepper Bacon-Wrapped Trout, 95
Rack of Lamb, 123
Smoked Artichokes, 139
Smoked Asparagus, 137
Smoked Lobster Tails, 102
Spicy Hickory-Smoked Barbecue Sauce, 163
Sugared Sea Bass, 101
Limes and lime juice
    Cuban Mojo-Marinated Pork, 66
    Smoked Corn on the Cob, 142
Lobster
    Scuppernong Lobster, 103
    Smoked Lobster Tails, 102
Low-and-slow smoking, 8

M

Maple syrup
    Carolina Mustard Sauce, 164
    Maple-Glazed Salmon, 96
    Mesquite Maple-Bacon Chicken, 51
    Pig Candy, 62
    Pineapple Pigtail, 116
Maraschino cherries
    Holiday Ham, 71
Marinades
    Smoky Teriyaki Marinade, 173
Masterbuilt smokers, 5–6
Meats. *See also Beef; Pork; Poultry*
    Big Fat Greek Fatty, 127
    Cajun Alligator Appetizer, 115
    Rack of Lamb, 123
    Smoked Venison Steaks, 114
    techniques and cuts, 111–112
Menus, 27–28
Milk. *See also* Buttermilk; Cream
    Hot-Smoked Gouda Bacon Dip, 154
    Smoked Mac and Cheese, 149

Mint
Rack of Lamb, 123
Molasses
Drunken Drumsticks, 42–43
Fireball Whiskey Meatballs, 77–78
Spicy Hickory-Smoked Barbecue Sauce, 163
Sweet Sriracha Barbecue Chicken, 44
Monterey Jack cheese
Smoked Mac and Cheese, 149
Mozzarella cheese
Fireball Whiskey Meatballs, 77–78
Smoked Tomato-Mozzarella Dip, 155

N

Nuts. *See also specific*
smoking, 148

O

Olives
Smoked Deviled Eggs, 141
Onions. *See also* Scallions
Bacon-Wrapped Crab-Stuffed Shrimp, 108
Big Fat Greek Fatty, 127
Big McFatty, 90
Breakfast Fatty, 119
Caramelized Honey Buffalo Chicken, 49
Cinnamon-Cured Fire-Smoked Chicken, 47
Cuban Mojo-Marinated Pork, 66
Drunken Drumsticks, 42–43
Fireball Whiskey Meatballs, 77–78
Loaded Hasselback Potatoes, 135
Pork Italian Sausage Fatty, 56
Smoked Bacon-Wrapped Onion Rings, 138
Smoked Beef Brisket Chili, 87
Smoked Brisket and Cheese Pizza, 91
Smoked Jalapeño Cheese-Stuffed Pork Balls, 64
Smoked Meat Loaf, 82
Smoked Onion Bombs, 133
Smoked Sausage Hash, 63
Smoked Stuffed Pumpkin Squash, 117
Smoky Brined Turkey, 48
Spicy Hickory-Smoked Barbecue Sauce, 163
Spicy Piggy Mac, 150

Stuffed Cornish Game Hens, 120
T-Bone Kebabs, 81
Oranges and orange juice
Citrus and Garlic Scallops, 106
Crispy-Skin Orange Chicken, 38
Cuban Mojo-Marinated Pork, 66
Stuffed Cornish Game Hens, 120
Oregano
Chimichurri Sauce, 169
Oysters
Smoky Oysters, 104

P

Pantry essentials, 23–24
Parmesan cheese
Fireball Whiskey Meatballs, 77–78
Smoked Brisket and Cheese Pizza, 91
Smoked Mac and Cheese, 149
Smoked Onion Bombs, 133
Smoked Tomato-Mozzarella Dip, 155
Smoky Oysters, 104
Parsley
Baba Ghanouj, 124
Big Fat Greek Fatty, 127
Buffalo Chicken Balls, 39
Chimichurri Sauce, 169
Drunken Drumsticks, 42–43
Fireball Whiskey Meatballs, 77–78
Lemon Pepper Bacon-Wrapped Trout, 95
Maple-Glazed Salmon, 96
Smoky Oysters, 104
Sugared Sea Bass, 101
Sweet Sriracha Barbecue Chicken, 44
Pasta
Smoked Mac and Cheese, 149
Spicy Piggy Mac, 150
Peaches
Smoked Peach Parfait, 121
Peanuts
Spicy Smoky Snack Mix, 156
Pecans
Glazed Spiced Pecans, 159
Hasselback Sweet Potatoes, 140

Smoked Brie with Brown Sugar and Pecans, 151
Pellet cookers, 5
Pineapple
    Holiday Ham, 71
    Pineapple–Brown Sugar Sauce, 168
    Pineapple Pigtail, 116
Poblano peppers
    Smoked Beef Brisket Chili, 87
    Smoked Chorizo-Stuffed Peppers, 122
Pork. *See also* Bacon
    Armadillo "Eggs," 126
    Baba Ghanouj, 125
    Breakfast Fatty, 119
    Carolina Pulled Pork Bites, 68
    Competition Baby Back Ribs, 58
    Cuban Mojo-Marinated Pork, 66
    cuts, 15, 53
    Fireball Whiskey Meatballs, 77–78
    Hickory-Smoked Pork Loin, 65
    Holiday Ham, 71
    Homemade Bacon, 61
    Peppercorn Pork Tenderloin, 57
    Porchetta Italian Pork Belly Roast, 118
    Pork Italian Sausage Fatty, 56
    Simple Smoked Pork Shoulder, 67
    Slow-Smoked Ancho Chile-Rubbed
        Boston Butt, 59–60
    Smoked Chorizo-Stuffed Peppers, 122
    Smoked Italian Sausage, 69
    Smoked Jalapeño Cheese-Stuffed Pork Balls, 64
    Smoked Meat Loaf, 82
    Smoked Pork Pinwheels, 70
    Smoked Sausage Hash, 63
    smoking chart, 14
    Spicy Piggy Mac, 150
    techniques, 53–55
Potatoes. *See also* Sweet potatoes
    Garlic-Rosemary Potato Wedges, 136
    Loaded Hasselback Potatoes, 135
    Potato Bacon Bites, 143
    Smoked Sausage Hash, 63
Poultry. *See also* Chicken; Turkey
    Herb-Smoked Quail, 37

Smoked Seasoned Duck, 113
    Stuffed Cornish Game Hens, 120
    techniques and cuts, 33–35
    washing, 35
Provolone cheese
    Smoked Brisket and Cheese Pizza, 91

Q
Queso fresco cheese
    Smoked Corn on the Cob, 142

R
Rice
    Stuffed Cornish Game Hens, 120
Rosemary
    Garlic-Rosemary Potato Wedges, 136
Rubs
    Bill's Best Barbecue Rub, 170
    Java Rub, 171

S
Safety
    electric smokers, 10–11
    food, 9, 18, 54
Salmon
    Maple-Glazed Salmon, 96
    smoked, 94
    Succulent Salmon Nuggets, 97
Sauces
    Alabama White Sauce, 167
    Carolina Mustard Sauce, 164
    Hot Pepper Vinegar Barbecue Sauce, 165
    pantry essentials, 24
    Pineapple–Brown Sugar Sauce, 168
    Plum Sauce, 172
    Spicy Hickory-Smoked Barbecue Sauce, 163
    tips for success, 162
Scallions
    Blue Cheese Cowboy Butter, 166
    Crab-Stuffed Tomato, 109
    Jamaican Jerk Chicken, 46
    Potato Bacon Bites, 143
    Smoked Tri-Tip Roast, 76

Spicy Korean Rib Eye Barbecue, 88
Scallops
    Citrus and Garlic Scallops, 106
    Smoked Shrimp and Scallops, 105
Seafood. *See also specific*
    cuts, 94
    smoking chart, 16
    techniques, 93–94
Seasoning, 34
Serrano peppers
    Hasselback Sweet Potatoes, 140
Sesame seeds
    Big Fat Greek Fatty, 127
    Big McFatty, 90
    Smoked Tri-Tip Roast, 76
Shrimp
    Bacon-Wrapped Crab-Stuffed Shrimp, 108
    Cajun Shrimp, 107
    Smoked Shrimp and Scallops, 105
Smoke roasting, 8
Smokers. *See* Electric smokers
Smoking
    about, 3–4
    bulk, 24–25
    foods for, 14, 16–18
    pantry essentials, 23–24
    steps, 19
    storing smoked foods, 25–26
    woods, 20–22
Sour cream
    Smoked Tomato-Mozzarella Dip, 155
Spatchcocking, 35
Spices, 23
Squash. *See also* Zucchini
    Smoked Spaghetti Squash, 144
    Smoked Stuffed Pumpkin Squash, 117
Sugar, 24
Sweet potatoes
    Hasselback Sweet Potatoes, 140

T
Tahini
    Baba Ghanouj, 124

Thermometers, 8–9
Thyme
    Applewood-Smoked Turkey Breast, 45
Tomatoes
    Big Fat Greek Fatty, 127
    Crab-Stuffed Tomato, 109
    Smoked Beef Brisket Chili, 87
    Smoked Brisket Grilled Cheese, 89
    Smoked Tomato-Mozzarella Dip, 155
    T-Bone Kebabs, 81
Tools and equipment, 8–9
Turkey
    Applewood-Smoked Turkey Breast, 45
    cuts, 34
    Garlic-Herb Turkey Legs, 40
    smoking chart, 16
    Smoky Brined Turkey, 48
    techniques, 34

V
Vegetables. *See also specific*
    smoking chart, 16–17
    techniques, 130

W
Wagyu beef, 74
Waiboer, Jack, 53
Whiskey
    Fireball Whiskey Meatballs, 77–78
    pairing, 28–29
Wine
    Smoked Seasoned Duck, 113
Woods, 20–22

Y
Yogurt
    Big Fat Greek Fatty, 127

Z
Zucchini
    T-Bone Kebabs, 81

BILL WEST is a country-music authority, barbecue enthusiast, and cookbook author based in Charleston, South Carolina. West is the on-air host and operations manager of Charleston's leading radio station, and has interviewed some of entertainment's biggest celebrities including Taylor Swift, Darius Rucker, Paula Deen, Zac Brown, Ryan Seacrest, Brad Paisley, Garth Brooks, Keith Urban, Carrie Underwood, and Alton Brown—just to name a few.

His blog, at BarbecueTricks.com, and YouTube channel have accumulated more than 2 million views and over 30 thousand subscribers.

A Chicago native, he is the youngest of six children and has spent the last 25 years in the Southeast playing country music on the radio. As a hobby, he competed in and judged barbecue competitions around the state for several years before he took up writing. Armed with a degree in broadcast journalism from Bradley University in Peoria, Illinois, he took his first "real job" in sunny Hilton Head Island, South Carolina, in 1989 (just one week before Hugo). Married for 23 years to his wife, MJ, they make their home in Charleston and have one guitar-playing son, Jack, who is 16 years old and just may be the next Brad Paisley or Keith Urban.

Download his free *Sauces & Sides* book:
BarbecueTricks.com/free-newsletter

Get his *BBQ Blueprint* book:
amzn.to/29xGMzD

@BillWestBS   facebook.com/BillWestBS